EL GRECO
BY L. GOLDSCHEIDER

PHAIDON

EL GRECO
BY L. GOLDSCHEIDER

PORTRAIT OF THE GRAND INQUISITOR DON FERNANDO DE GUEVARA. About 1598. New York, Metropolitan Museum (76⅜ × 51¼)

EL GRECO

PAINTINGS · DRAWINGS AND SCULPTURES

BY LUDWIG GOLDSCHEIDER

WITH TWO HUNDRED PLATES

THE PHAIDON PRESS · LONDON

FIRST EDITION 1938
SECOND EDITION 1949
THIRD EDITION 1954

COLOUR PLATES PRINTED BY HUNT BARNARD AND CO LTD · AYLESBURY
MONOCHROME PLATES PRINTED BY WAGNER'SCHE UNIVERSITÄTS-BUCHDRUCKEREI · INNSBRUCK
TEXT PRINTED BY HUNT BARNARD AND CO LTD · AYLESBURY

DOMENIKOS THEOTOKOPOULOS
CALLED EL GRECO

A DARK ISLAND in the Hellenic Sea, equally remote from Europe, Asia, and Africa, equally accessible to Greeks, Egyptians, and Syrians – the island of Dionysus, the home of the ancient legends of Prometheus and Daedalus: such is Crete, the birthplace of Domenikos Theotokopoulos. A thousand years before the flowering of Greek art, this island produced an art all of its own, at the perfection of which we may guess from the ruins of it that remain: immense labyrinthine palaces of exquisite and graceful decoration; columns that swell upward; female ivory figurines, variegated and ornamented with gold, tightly corseted and with wide-opened eyes; elongated clay figures of animals and springers; landscape frescoes in blue and yellow, full of butterflies and sharply defined flowers; fairylike pictures with blue crocus-gatherers or mauve-coloured elongated figures of youths with vessels between wide-spread fingers – all this the scattered shards of a great and overripe art, the remote source of the art of El Greco. What vestiges remain to us from this early period are as eloquent as they are scanty; but the further we progress through the centuries, the dimmer are the witnesses to the artistic life on Greco's native isle. Egyptians, Greeks, and Romans, colonists from Byzantium and Palestine, Saracens and Crusaders from all lands touched at this island, lived or lodged there for a longer or shorter time, and brought with them their art: always different peoples, always a different art. And it almost seems that a note from all these various melodies of art has been woven into the music of the art of Domenikos Theotokopoulos. His early portraits seem Venetian, like those of his teachers, but his later and riper are more akin to the painters of El Fayum than to Tintoretto: the construction and the expression of his sacred pictures grew ever more Byzantinian with the years; his increasingly elongated and sinuous forms seem to find their way back to Early Gothic illumination; but to the Spaniards he remained always El Greco, the Greek. In Venice he was Venetian; the Roman Mannerists regarded him as one of themselves. Yet in his mature period, as the Greek of Toledo, he discovered painting once more for himself, as an art he had made all his own, that he had learnt from no one, and that he could transmit to no one, an art unsuitable to reproduce this visible world, but apt to record the world of his own visions.

Phodele, a village nestling between cliffs, near the sea and near Candia, the capital of Crete, is now named as the painter's birthplace, and 1541 is said to be the year of his birth. In Greco's lifetime Crete, 'the Queen of the Isles', belonged to Venice; and Venice was under permanent obligation to defend her against the Turks, who later, some half-century after Greco's death, wrested her from the Venetians, after pillaging the coasts of the island for five generations. In the year 1566 the danger was imminent; Chios and Naxos had already fallen; and it was perhaps in this year that Greco removed to Venice. This city was intersected by the sea and therefore not uncongenial to the island youth; its architecture was just sufficiently touched by the East to be intelligible in its grandeur to the young Byzantine painter, but all its churches, palaces, and dwellings teemed with such wealth of true painting as to strike him with amazement and despair at the spectacle of such high art.

Greco proceeded to study his art. About twenty-five years of age, really too old for an Italian workshop, at first glance he was not specially gifted, as he necessarily lacked what a Venetian youth would have absorbed from childhood merely with his eyes, and he was dowered with an originality which, without prevision of its subsequent development, could only be considered as a defect. He entered Titian's workshop, perhaps also those of the Bassani and Tintoretto. Titian was then no longer the master of bright and riotous colours, the painter of languorous Venetian Venuses and of bacchanal landscapes. His colours had become as dark as his themes (but the palette of the whole world was then beginning to darken), he was painting the sufferings of St. Lawrence and of St. Sebastian, and the sufferings of Our Lord at the crowning with thorns and on the Cross. During those years a Council was in session, in order to save the Faith, threatened from the East by the armies of the Koran and more violently from the North by the doctrines of Luther. Painting, the prophetic among the arts, always the first to divine changes in world conditions, began at that time to place its figures in rooms that were as dark as dungeons or torture-chambers. And the fire which the Inquisition never let die down, flared up in the pictures of St. Lawrence the Martyr; the luminous visions of the mystics were reflected in artistic lighting effects against asphalt-black backgrounds; and the strict rules of Ignatius Loyola recur in the inquisitorial directions of contemporary painter's primers.

The young Greco copied Titian; two pictures are preserved, a *Mater dolorosa* and a female portrait. From the content of all Titian's paintings he absorbed so much as never to become free therefrom. Greco was then painting on little wooden panels, not on canvas like the Venetians.[1] An *Adoration of the Shepherds* of Jacopo Bassano he copied in several versions. In his brush-work he tried to approach Tintoretto, from whom he learnt much, not only drawing from wax and clay dolls, of which a large number was found among his belongings after death.

On the 16th November 1570 the Croatian miniature-painter, Georg Julius Glovicic, called Julio Clovio in Italy, wrote to Cardinal Alessandro Farnese in Viterbo: 'A young Candiote has appeared in Rome, a pupil of Titian, who, so far as I can judge, is unique in painting; among other things, he has painted a self-portrait that confounds all the painters in Rome.' And he begged the Cardinal to reserve a room in his palace for the young artist. This self-portrait has disappeared, although there has come down to us a number of other paintings which he executed for the Cardinal and for his librarian, the Canonicus Fulvio Orsini, of which the most original is a fantastic picture of Sinai (Plate 10) and the finest the portrait of his patron Clovio (Plate 5). One has only to compare Clovio's self-portrait[2] with Greco's portrait of him, in order to perceive that the Greek had nothing to learn from the miniature-painter, unless it were miniature-painting itself, of which a few examples exist from a later period (Plates 65, 66). His art of portraiture draws its primary strength from Tintoretto and Paolo Veronese. His spiritual fathers he has placed like a large signature in the right-hand corner of an early version of *The Cleansing of the Temple* (Plates 3 and 4): Titian, Michelangelo, and Raphael, by the side of Clovio. Traces of Raphael's *School of Athens* may long be

---

1. One of the earliest works of this kind is the so-called Modena triptych, bearing the signature 'Dominikos' in Greek capitals. It is now in the Galleria Estense at Modena.

2. From the Ambraser Collection in the Kunsthistorisches Museum at Vienna. The inscription in the background runs: *Julius Clouius Croatus sui ipsius effigiator A(nn)o aetat : 30. salut. 1528.*

detected in his work; Michelangelo's own tomb he freely imitated in his *Pietà* (Plate 8); but what he drew from him above all was courage for the boldness of form. Then he copied Taddeo Zuccari's *Adoration of the Shepherds*, inspected Salviati's frescoes so closely that their influence upon him was evident forty years later, and copied Correggio's *Night*.[3]

Until 1576 Greco remained in Italy. Perhaps it was then and there (if not later in Toledo) that he met Cervantes, who had fought in the Battle of Lepanto and lost an arm; perhaps, loving music as he did, he had got to know Palestrina, who in his time was master of the Vatican choir; perhaps, too, the magician Giambattista della Porta, the inventor of the camera obscura.

But whatever Rome could offer Greco in personalities and works, Rome was no longer the focus of the spiritual world; the new spirit, borne by the fanatical discipline of Loyola and by the ecstatic extravagance of St. Teresa of Avila, settled there where the Escorial was built as the new citadel of faith, and in the palaces of Toledo, which were converted into monasteries, like houses into fortresses in times of danger. Philip the Second was more Catholic than the Pope, Toledo more ecclesiastical than Rome.

This Spanish Lhassa, in which 150,000 people then dwelt, had hundreds of monasteries, and new ones were added every year. Laws which were passed against them remained ineffectual. Although Toledo was a busy place, the city of the most flexible sword-blades, of the finest silk fabrics, of the most artistic tiles – all these activities were grouped around the Palace of the Archbishop, who, next to the Emperor, was the most powerful man in the land, around the thousand monasteries, where death and not life was the chief concern, around the square in front of the Puerta del Cambrón, the execution-ground of the Tribunal of the Inquisition. 'The masters of Toledo are the priests,' Navagiero, Venice's Ambassador to the Emperor, had written. And just as we are not shocked to see a person executed for high treason, so that age was not shocked to see traitors to the Lord of Lords executed. It was a matter of belief. People believed in God, and people believed there was such a thing as treachery to God. People believed then, as ever, in the justice of punishment and in the beneficence of cruelty. And all these fires and prayers and bells, and the walls which cribbed, cabined, and confined earthly life, exhorted the people to do battle heroically for the highest: for life eternal. This gigantic spiritual fortress of Toledo was at war with the world for God.

Christ as warrior: such was the conception of the soldier Loyola. And the saints, those fallen soldiers of faith, arose from their graves and the shrines of relics, no longer like coloured symbols as in Italy, but as embodied visions in the midst of the Spanish people. Like every strong faith, this, too, gave birth to a strong art. Italian art had believed in beauty, and thus had seen beauty everywhere. Spanish art believed in holiness, and thus saw it in the flesh as it had never been seen before. Visions of beauty were replaced by visions of holiness.

But at the time when Greco settled in Spain, national Spanish painting did not yet exist, or rather was lost in imitation of the magnificent achievements of all peoples. In

3. Fra Francisco de los Santos mentions another copy by El Greco of a Correggio painting in his '*Descripción del Real Monasterio de San Lorenzo del Escorial*', Madrid 1657 (English translation: *Description of the Royal Palace and Monastery of the Escorial*, from the Spanish of Fray Francisco de los Santos, by George Thompson, London 1760, p. 186): '*Another (picture) represents the Holy Virgin with the divine infant, and St. Catherine and St. Sebastian sitting with her. This is supposed to be a copy from Correggio, though I rather believe it to be from (Antonio) Acorezo. The copyer is known to be Domenico Greco.*'

their empire of Catholic imperialism, founded by Charles the Fifth, shaped by Philip the Second, the sun of art did not set, but as yet the starlight of native individuality had not touched Spanish soil. This empire was too vast, too many people skilled in art inhabited it; Holland, Flanders, and a good slice of Italy belonged to it, and thence came artists and thither went Spaniards ever since the days of Van Eyck, in order to learn, which they did only too completely, forgetting their own ways. Pupils of Leonardo da Vinci there were, like Ferrando de Llanos and Ferrando Yañez, pupils of Titian, like El Mudo. Sánchez Coello and Pantoja de la Cruz painted portraits of the Spanish nobility, but they were not far removed from Anthonis Mor, the Netherlandish court painter of Philip the Second. Titian served both great kings, Tintoretto's pictures were brought to decorate the Escorial, together with pictures of many lesser Italian artists, and the artists themselves specially summoned by Philip; Netherlanders were there, too, with their fantastic conceptions of Hell, which they had imbibed from the work of Hieronymus Bosch, and with their faithful and sober art of portraiture. The native tendency, archaically inclined towards Gothic, produced little except the pictures of Luis de Morales of Estremadura, called el Divino, the divine.

In the spring of 1577 El Greco came to Toledo. Two years later, during a lawsuit about a fee, he was asked why he had come, and declined to answer. Perhaps he had already made the contract for the altar of San Domingo in letters written from Rome to Toledo, perhaps he had only been lured by the hope of helping to decorate the Escorial. He had brought with him an assistant, Francisco Prevoste, and his uncle, Manusso Theotocopuli Griego. Toledo must have seemed more congenial to him than Rome; here he found the pines and olives of his native isle again, and the Mohammedan East in many buildings, melodies, and customs; even the grey cliffs and the rushing of the waters, in a more compressed and violent form. Greco was enamoured of this city, perched on a high bare rock, up which the houses climb like jutting stones, surrounded by a deep abyss, through which the Tagus drives its waters.

Greco was never tired of painting this rock city, in a vast landscape, in the background of the *Laocoön*, behind attitudinizing saints and the towering Cross. Toledo became Gethsemane. Clouds hover above the ash-grey stony land, slashed like the curtain of which it is written that at the hour of Christ's death it was rent in twain; grey storm light lies on the meadows, which tumble down to the Tagus; the dust, driven by the breath of the storm, is laid on the green earth like the dust of the charnel-house. In the greyness of this menacing, rocky wilderness Greco found himself, just as Dürer found himself in the blueness of Italy.

In Toledo Greco was able to meet compatriots from Crete, like Michel Carcandilos and the poet Antonio Calosynas; Cretans were illuminating the missals for the Escorial church. Greco, who was then certainly ignorant of the Spanish tongue, approached Italian artists in Toledo, such as Pompeo Leone, whom he painted at work on the King's bust. Don Diego de Castilla, deacon of Toledo Cathedral, who had the placing of the order for the altar of Santo Domingo el Antiguo, seems to have been one of the first Spaniards whom Greco attracted to his circle. He portrayed him on the left-hand side of the altar, in white and pale-gold Easter robes (Plates 14 and 19). Greco laboured two years at this altar, his first great work. From little wooden panels and modest canvas surfaces he had passed to working in huge dimensions. *The Assumption of the Virgin*, as centre picture of the high altar, and *The Trinity*, attached to the attica of the altar, to show the celestial occurrence in the uppermost regions above the ascension of the Virgin close to the earth, measured together twenty-three feet (Plates 12 and 13). Larger than life are the two Johns (Plates 21–22) at the side of the altar, like the figures of saints which Tintoretto had painted for the Biblioteca Marciana, which also have the effect of coloured reproductions of sculptures. *The Assumption of the Virgin* (Plate 13) recalls a wood-carving of Alonso Cano, the Christ in the clouds reminds one of Michelangelo's Roman and Florentine *Pietà* (Plate 12), despite the use made of a woodcut by Dürer. The whole of this altar is conceived plastically; even the architecture and the sculptural decoration originated from Greco's designs. Owing much to various traditions of art and to many schools, this altar-piece is yet entirely Greco. The way in which he suggests motion in the right half of *The Assumption* (Plate 13), in the congested group of six figures, from the kneeling man in the foreground to the half-bent man in the centre and the four erect figures in the background, leading the eye through the lines of the folds in the garments and the lines of the curved limbs from the bottom right-hand corner to the centre above – all this is without prototype. Jerónima de las Cuebas, his beloved, whose features shine forth from so many sacred pictures, and whom he immortalized, in youth and age, in his two finest portraits of women (Plates 53 and 108), probably sat as model for the Madonna in *The Adoration of the Shepherds* (Plate 15) in the right transept. For the infant Christ he could have drawn from the cradle his own son, Jorge Manuel,[4] who was born to him of Jerónima in 1578, about the time this picture originated.

Contemporary with the San Domingo altar-piece there was finished the *Espolio de las vestiduras* (Plate 27), ordered in a contract dated the 2nd July 1577 for the *Vestuario*, the vestry of the priests, by the Toledo Cathedral Chapter. Just as the Last Supper was the proper theme for a wall-picture in the refectory of a monastery, so this scene, which depicts the disrobing of Christ, was appropriate to an ecclesiastical vestry. But it was a mediaeval theme, alien from the Renaissance painters. Greco's picture excited controversy; he was obliged to bring a lawsuit in connection with his *Espolio*. Priestly experts took exception to the fact that the heads of the two thieves, and also the heads of the soldiers and of the people, were higher than the head of Christ, and that the three Marys were standing close by, although the Gospel states that they had looked on from afar. But the Commission decided that 'the painting is inestimable, so great is its value'. Just as Greco's self-portrait had quickly made him famous nine years before in Rome, so his *Espolio* now brought him rapid fame in Toledo. All his life Greco was impelled to repeat this picture, in smaller and larger variants, which show the development of his brush-work, and in variants in oblong shape, without the Marys and the myrmidon boring holes. Workshop replicas have also been preserved, as well as contemporary copies made by foreign hands. In this picture repose and excitement are strangely blended, in the expression of the lines and the values of the colours. Madder lake reinforced by black dominates the centre of the picture and sparkles over the yellow and bluish greys of the faces, of the armour and of the sky. The picture is vertically articulated like a Gothic church; the halberd handles continue the movement as far as the upper edge of the picture. The flat depth, upon which the picture is pressed like a sarcophagus relief,

4. Jorge Manuel became an architect and a painter. He married several times, appears to have led a gay life, contracted debts and even got put in prison. He died in poverty on 29th March 1631. The only certain work by him is a signed copy of his father's 'Espolio'.

9

makes the motions seem larger. In its dramatic intensity the painting has the effect of a silent moment in a Passion Play.

The same period of creative activity saw a number of other important paintings, like the *Saint Sebastian* at Palencia (Plate 11), and the *Sudary of St. Veronica* (Plate 37). The *Sebastian*, an impressive and monumental figure, is sketched in a bold anatomy and modelled with a flickering shading; head and hand are too small, the size of the limbs boldly exaggerated, constructive curves are inserted as expressive values. The first deliberate 'deformations' are in evidence here; in the colouring, abstract white and black begin to dominate. For the *Veronica* Greco used the same model as for one of the Marys in the Espolio, but the degree of naturalism varies considerably in these two contemporary renderings (Plates 36 and 37).

The picture, glittering like enamel, which represents the adoration of the Sign of Christ in the Heavens and on Earth (Plate 40), has been called *El sueño de Felipe II*, the King's Dream, and in fact it can only be understood as a reflection of the shadowy light, the iridescent colours, the incoherent flight of details, and the convincing improbability of a dream. Here the abyss of earth calls to the abyss of heaven. In an aerial landscape, which consists of rolling clouds like a naked mountain of rocks, a sulphurous yellow and golden abyss is opening, in which the sacred monogram, the badge of the Jesuit Order, is planted. The whitish light, which pours out of this crater, floods the hovering angels, who are black as blocks of basalt where they are untouched by the light. A cloud half conceals, like a piece of stage scenery, two large angel shapes; angels kneel on ascending clouds as on a theatrical device, and a cloud casts its great shadows upon the earth beneath. There below, straight through the shadows, from the confused light of bluish-grey and yellow depths, a mighty procession of saints is streaming towards the foreground of the picture; their foreheads gleaming white like the crest of waves. In the centre, kneeling in a triangle, are three praying figures: Philip the Second, a black silhouette; the Spanish Pope, grey and red, with red gloves; and Charles the Fifth, in a yellow mantle with white and black ermine. Gold cushions and carpets, which bring out the King's black in strong relief, are multi-coloured as the jewel-studded lid of a Byzantine casket of relics. Grey and blackish-blue, in the right foreground, yawns wide the mouth of hell, black and sulphurous yellow inside, and it is discharging a flood of human limbs, fleshly as on Charon's boat in Michelangelo's *Last Judgement*, half-decomposed limbs and living skeletons. Behind this gaping abyss there flows, in uncertain lights, a molten stream, into which the damned are cast; on the centre bank stands a catacomb, golden and fiery, with black gallows, from which tiny human bodies are dangling.

This picture, full of the spirit of the early Jesuits, found its way to Philip's Escorial. And then at length Greco received his first commission from the King: to paint a representation of the legend of St. Maurice (Plate 44).

Brooding perpetually upon death and life eternal, like the kings of Egypt when they were building their pyramids, Philip the Second went on constructing his Escorial, which, in the rigid outlines of St. Lawrence's gridiron, was to be at one and the same time monastery, church, burial-vault, and palace. Unlike his great father, who was perpetually travelling about his vast realm, in order to rule and to wage war, he sat imprisoned in the poorest chamber of his castle, whence he transacted all business, decided everything himself, even the most trivial details, dictated, wrote with his own hand; no detail was too petty for him to leave to others, not even instructions to the lowest officials; in this, too, he was unlike his father, who thought only on broad lines. This king, without personal contact but full of decisions; without people because full of mistrust; ruler of an immense empire which he never saw; who knew air only as it percolated into his Spanish chamber, light only as it filtered through his window-panes; this invisible king, whose sword flashed over the whole world; this most sensual of all Spaniards filled with hatred of the earthly; unhealthy, weak, and ever shivering, yet tireless: he could carry the burden to the last that was too heavy for his strong father. The empire was sick, and he was for ever bent on healing it with iron and fire. But blood had to be paid for with gold, and the countries had become poor. Gold came in shiploads from the American colonies, but the effect of this was only to make gold cheap and the caballeros and citizens poor who possessed the scanty supplies of old gold. The war taxes pressed almost to starvation point, only the monks and the beggars were careless and free in their propertyless condition, and so people took refuge in the monasteries and in poverty. The monasteries were wealthy, but not the monks; festivals were sumptuous, but miserable was the working day. Complicated laws were passed to increase exports, to restrict imports; gold and silver could not leave the country at all; and poverty deepened. People and books were burnt, the orthodoxy of art strictly controlled, Jews and Moors expelled from the country; moral and economic disintegration went on apace. At the time when Greco died, the city of Toledo addressed a complaint to the King that whole streets were deserted, entire handicrafts had died out, and sites were worthless. It came to such a pass that collections were taken up from house to house for the Treasurer of the Spanish King, and collecting boxes were rattled in the streets. But this declension, which had begun with the retreat of Charles the Fifth to San Yuste, was so slow as to be imperceptible, whereas the empire expanded and was accompanied by an effulgence of the arts that dazzled contemporaries, and their successors glorified the century. Next to religion, Philip the Second loved art, but nothing else. He did not love himself, whom he esteemed only as the ruler of the empire, and he loved his dynasty only to the extent that he saw in it the preservers of this power. In the midst of his writing drudgery, he found time to encourage the arts, as builder and as collector of pictures. He even found time to try his skill as amateur painter. He loved above all the masters of Venice: Titian, Veronese, and Tintoretto. In his early Toledo works, Greco had not completely broken away from those Venetian painters who were his teachers, and thus was commissioned by Philip to paint the legend of St. Maurice.

When the picture was finished, the King rejected it. Philip failed to recognize his own painter, the artist who had painted as the King was thinking, as the foremost painter of Catholic imperialism. 'The picture does not please His Majesty,' wrote Sigüenza, 'and that is no wonder, for it pleases few, although they say that there is much art in it and its author understands much, and there are excellent things of his to be seen.' The picture is composed of the colours ultramarine blue, madder lake, and bright ochre; together with grey, white and black, and light green; its linear composition is based on a network of zig-zag lines: the edges of the clouds, the curves of the angels, the spiral groupings of the martyrs on three levels, the chain of arms. It is not the naturalistic details in this picture (convincing portraits and still plant life in the foreground, often compared with Dürer's *Lawn*) that affect us so; the stimulating effect proceeds entirely from the restless zig-zag composition and a similar play of the three dominant colours, upon an asymmetry which holds all the weights as on oscillating scales.

The exciting quality of this picture is in keeping with the excitements of the time. The counter-reformation was then in full swing; science and mysticism were disputing which was the proper conception of the universe; in this decade appeared the chief writings of Giordano Bruno and the *Book of Life* of Saint Teresa; Juan de la Cruz composed his god-intoxicated poems; Valdes, Rogete, and their successors constructed spectacles and telescopes and pushed man's sight beyond its natural limits; the study of the circulation of the blood, the knowledge of the eye, zoology, and botany, everything was forging ahead; Hernández began to study American archaeology; the Jesuits, the civilization of the Chinese; a new interest in the exotic began to be perceptible, imitations of Chinese porcelain were made in Toledo; new stimulants also came from abroad, like tobacco and coffee.

The two chief sciences remained theology and humanism, the doctrines of the true divinity and of the true humanity. El Greco, a 'thinking' artist, was addicted to both sciences, as may be inferred from the library mentioned in the inventory of his effects. This catalogue comprises seventy-two books, including the Bible, Basilius and John Chrysostom, Homer, Euripides, Demosthenes, Lucian, and Aesop. Greco knew four languages – Greek, Latin, Italian, and Spanish: that, too, is proved by the catalogue. The painter Pacheco, Velázquez's father-in-law, who visited Greco in 1611, mentions a treatise on art by Greco, an essay which has so far not been unearthed: if we had it, we should know more about the range of Greco's culture. At any rate, this work seems mainly to have dealt with architecture, and, if Pacheco's art book is any criterion, Greco's book would also contain discussions of a theological character.

Greco's external life, like that of many a Spanish hidalgo, was dominated by pomp and poverty. We hear of unusual fees, of a house-rent ten times greater than that of his neighbours; but we hear, too, of lawsuits and debts; his wardrobe was knightly and poor: a cloth cloak, a calico cloak, a pair of hose, a silk costume, a hat, a sword, a dagger, and a pair of spurs – that is all he left behind at his death. In the palace of the Marqués de la Villena, in the former Jewish quarter, he occupied twenty-four rooms, but his furniture, as enumerated in the inventory of his estate, seems to have been barely sufficient to furnish a couple of rooms.

Greco moved into this palace of Villena in the year 1585, at the time he started painting *The Entombment of Count Orgaz* (Plates 54–63). The contract is dated the 18th March 1586, and the work was to be finished by Christmas of that year.

This is a representation of the miracle which is supposed to have happened when the Knight Orgaz was being buried in the church of San Tomé: Saints Augustine and Stephen were said to have appeared and relieved the priests of their work. In the colours of a stormy sky, in grey and yellow, white and black, Greco painted this miracle. The yellow in the garments of both saints has the same unearthly light as the yellow of the cloud-edges in the arch; the black in the clothes of the chain of spectators gives the foreground the same relief-depth as the abrupt black beside the hard whites in the upper regions. Like the contour of a violently rising and falling wave is the outline of the four illuminated figures in the foreground: steeply upwards and downwards about the grey monk on the left, in mutually inclined curves about the yellow of the two saints, and again steeply upwards and downwards about the white figure, his back towards the spectator, of the priest on the right. The depth of the wave indicates the optical centre; the double curve of the saints' yellow garments is carried by the greyish-white of the shroud down still farther; in this lowest depth rests the bluish-grey armour of the knight. This line-movement in the lower plane corresponds with a line moving in the opposite sense in the upper vault, but even stronger than the movement of the outlines is the colour-movement of yellow and black above and beneath. This purely technical restlessness has a counterpoise in the rigid repose of the content. Like pale pillars of salt, all the figures and torch-flames and cloud-shapes seem to congeal in one everlasting moment, and even the five astonished hands are motionless as the gestures of harshly illuminated sculpture. The division between the upper and the lower spheres in this ceremonial picture of Spanish piety is less than that between fore-ground and background. The miracle is displayed in its whole force, not as something supernatural, but as a supremely natural event; the priests and the nobles, the pious elements in the Spanish nation, are present at the occurrence on the firm ground of the Church; and above, in the firm region of the clouds, are the saints, the nobles of the Kingdom of Heaven.

The picture of the Orgaz entombment contains a plenitude of portraits. In earlier paintings, too, like the *Martyrdom of St. Maurice* (Plates 43 and 45), models were employed for portraiture; but they transcended the individual and were deftly woven into the composition. In *The Entombment of Count Orgaz* the portraits retain their full individual character, so much so as to arouse perpetual curiosity concerning the names of the persons represented. The intention here seems to be the contrary of that which the Protestant North later strove to attain: Frans Hals's groups of musketeers, Rembrandt's *Night Watch*, give groups of portraits in the form of narrative; in the Orgaz picture the portraits of contemporaries are introduced into a legend without re-casting it. Through this group of naturalistic portraits the Catholic miracle story of the Entombment of Count Orgaz receives its worldly attestation, just as the Dutch portrait groups by stylistic transformation touch with poetry the burgher world.

The portraits in this painting have all the qualities of Greco's art of portraiture. Justi found the portraits by the hand of Greco 'corpse-like in colouring, shadowy in model-ling'. Others again have been struck by the somnambulism in the expression of the faces, the ascetic and the ecstatic, the cruel and the passionate, kept under by self-repression and outward coldness, a nervous laceration, suggesting Toledo blades, so sharp as in course of time to penetrate the sheaths in which they rest. Others again have emphasized the colourlessness of the portraits, the night-dark backgrounds, into which the black garments and the grey and olive-green faces melt. But Greco's best portrait, that of the Grand Inquisitor, is at the same time one of his pictures that are strongest in colour (Frontispiece). What is common to all these portraits is only their impressionistic quality, which in the later period is strikingly reminiscent of the technique of Dutch contemporaries (Plate 94), their freedom from deliberate 'distortions', their relative naturalism. Greco painted saints quite differently, even when he treated their faces like portraits; his hidalgos and priests he painted as they appeared to the eye, in an earthly light; the others as visions, in unearthly, phosphorescent illumination. As a comparison, the portrait of an unknown man in Minneapolis (Plate 185) is approximately con-temporary with that of *St. Bernard* in the Greco Museum (Plate 153). The portrait is like a face caught in a flat mirror, while the picture of the saint seems as if caught in a billowy convex mirror, which makes the two halves of the face unequal, all the contours being distorted into ovals; the treatment of the shadows corresponds in the one case to the strong light of the afternoon, in the other case to the uncertain hues of twilight. *The Lady with the Golden Flower in her Hair* was perhaps also the model for the *Madonna Caritatis* in Illescas; here, too, the distinction between visualization and vision becomes a distinction in the treatment of form (Plates 86 and 152).

These linear stylizations, soon after Greco's death, gave rise to the legend of his madness, and in our century to the legend of his astigmatism. The fact is overlooked that, in all his creative periods, Greco was normal and normal-sighted when he wanted to be, that is, in his portraits; and that he deliberately distorted his drawing, like a Mannerist, when he intended to do so, that is, when he was representing supernatural figures. *The Entombment of Count Orgaz* already exhibits these qualities: close to nature in the lower, earthly groups, remote from nature in the higher, heavenly. The nude figure of John the Baptist (Plate 54), kneeling opposite the Madonna on the cloud, would make eleven head-lengths if erect. The rest of the saints are not drawn much differently than in his later apostles. And in *The Stoning of St. Stephen* (Plate 59), below in the hem of the saint's robe, we find the same forms of the nude as much later in *Laocoön* or in *The Fifth Seal* (Plates 193 and 194).

In many respects the altar-piece of St. Joseph's Chapel in Toledo (Plates 112, 113, 122) is a return to Venetian forms of expression, with the charming angels and putti, the hint of Colleone, the more plastic modelling, the warmer colours. The standing figures are elongated in a manner that recalls the Gothic figures of saints at the abbey of Moissac, or the proportions in the mosaics of Ravenna. Similar in attitude and conception to the *St. Joseph* is *St. James*, treated like a statue (Plate 109); and the bronze-like *St. Bernard* (Plate 151), as well as the gleaming *Ildefonso* (Plate 110), the *St. Peter*, towering like a monumental stone figure (Plate 158), and *St. Augustine*, producing the effect of a draped wooden statue (Plate 179), show Greco's sculptural instincts; much more in these paintings than in his sculptures, of which many are attested by documents: the decoration for the High Altar of San Domingo (1579), the *Donation of the Chasuble*, as decoration to the *Espolio*, carved with his own hand (Plate 26), the *Madonna with the Rosary* in the parish church of Talavera (1591), the figures of Hope and Faith in the church of La Caridad at Illescas (1603–1606), the more than life-size saints and the little *Resurrected Christ* in the Hospital of Afuera (Plate 189). Like a great plastic group Greco also constructed his *Pietà* (Plate 69), and his *Madonna Sheltering the Faithful under Her Cloak* (Plate 150). If all these pictures remind one of sculpture in the round, his later altar-paintings suggest the representation method of relief.

Ecstasy was defined by Immanuel Hermann Fichte as 'farsight with the overcoming of sensual perception in space and time'. Greco's great paintings in the Prado are ecstatic visions, in an unearthly light, with dreamlike distortions of forms, released from earthly perceptions (Plates 74, 115, 118, 171). Mystics have spoken of luminous apparitions, poets have continually sought to reproduce dream faces in words: Greco caught the visions of those in ecstasy and the magic imagery of the dreamers in line and colour, in exact recollection of the experience and without assimilation to the visible world. From the moment of the 'overcoming of sensual perception' Greco's paintings are filled with an optical content which cannot be further explained, which defies all the laws of composition and colour and can no longer be tested by the proportions and optics of the tangible and visible world.

However, there is a certain development in his painting, from *The Resurrection of Christ* to *The Pentecost* (Plates 118 and 171), from the sequence of paintings in Illescas (Plates 150, 181), to the late versions of *The Adoration of the Shepherds* and *The Mount of Olives* (cf. Plates 139 and 191). Greco's style achieved its zenith in the works that he left unfinished when he died on the 6th April 1614: in *The Baptism of Christ* in the Hospital of San Juan Bautista (Plate 204) and *The Betrothal of the Virgin* in Foïshor Castle (Plates 200–202).

From this uncompleted picture Greco's painting technique can be most easily studied. In nearly all his pictures the canvas is covered with a bolus groundwork, which is usually red, but sometimes of a brownish, sometimes of a yellowish-red hue. This priming is not painted over everywhere, but remains in places untouched, both in shadow and in light. Sometimes Greco used coloured canvas, mostly of medium brown tone, as in an early portrait in Copenhagen; sometimes white grounding, upon which the first body colours were laid in red-brown tempera.[5] In every case Greco painted from dark into light. He painted with a whitish paste, a thick resinous oil-colour, transparent where it is laid on thinly, and semi-transparent where it is more pastose. Upon the red-brown groundwork, therefore, there is this single colour, applied thickly or thinly, a great wealth of tones and the whole modelling from white to grey and grey-brown. The primary painting of the Impressionists requires a full palette, in order to reproduce similarly the tones obtained by transparency. Upon these first body colours lies a second coating in white and black, with a thick, pastose ochre for the middle tones. Into these pictures, fully traced and modelled throughout by the under-painting, the local colours are introduced as transparent glazes, broadly applied, very fluid and passing lightly over places of varying transparency. As with the second coat of body colours, so in the case of the local colours, the same brush-work produces quite different colour-effects without mingling and without any break.

Greco's later works, such as his *Laocoön* and the *Opening of the Fifth Seal* (Plates 200 and 201), can perhaps be explained in their technique, but not in their visible content, that is in their spirit. As dreams have their coherence and their reason, which yet are not the causal connection and the logic of waking, so these pictures have their own linear and colour organism. For these limb-twistings and elongations there is no wherefore, for these black and coloured shadows, for this quivering storm no other meaning than the impression they create.

The peculiarities of Greco's later style have always been recognized for what they are, even in times when they were in disfavour. A hundred years ago Gautier observed: 'Thin sharp lines which traverse the shadow parts like so many sword-blades'; and more than half a century ago Carl Justi wrote words of blame that sound to us like

5. This double priming, red over white, was formerly well known and in general use, not only in Venice, but also in Northern Europe; it may even have been known to Antiquity. – In Henry Peacham's *Complete Gentleman*, 1622 (Chapter XIII, p. 130), we find the same receipt: 'First, for your table whereupon to draw your picture, plane it very even, and with size (made of glue sodden long in faire water, till the glue be quite dissolved) mingled and heat with Spanish white finely ground, white it over; then let it dry, then white it over again, and so the third time, then being dry, scrape it very even with a sharpe knife till it be smooth, then prime it with red lead or some other colour.' – Henry Fuseli, who used oil priming for his own paintings, believed that a similar double priming was used in Greek painting (*Lectures on Painting*, London 1801): 'A plane or tablet, primed with white, and then covered with what they called Punic wax, first amalgamated with a tough resinous pigment, generally of a red, sometimes dark brown, or black colour.'

praise: 'In the grip of a heavy dream he seems to drive the brush, exhibiting the distorted incubus of his overheated brain as revelation. With feverish fingers he creates model figures as if out of rubber, in twelvehead-lengths, which he hangs up in front of him; with wild flourishes, without modelling or outline, on one plane, but in marvellous symmetrical arrangement, with water-blue and sulphur-yellow as his favourite colours, finally with white and blackish violet, he hurls them on to the canvas.' The new century, which has re-learnt the language of Byzantine art and that of the 'Primitives', has discovered El Greco as the spirit of Spanish art; but for us he is even more: one of the perfect religious painters of this world.

London, 1938   LUDWIG GOLDSCHEIDER

Statues of Faith, Hope and Charity. By Monegro after El Greco's designs, Toledo, Santo Domingo el Antiguo

NOTES ON SOME OF THE PLATES

Plates 1 and 105 : In his *El Greco,* Berlin 1931, p. 11, A. L. Mayer discusses in detail the question of Greco's portraits of himself. He rejects Cossio's assertion that the picture in Parma is a self-portrait and accepts as self-portraits only the head next to the man with a flag, in the 'Martyrdom of St. Maurice' (Plate 43), another head in the 'Burial of Count Orgaz' (Plate 63) and the portrait in New York (Plate 141). On p. 72, however, he says that the head of Christ on the 'Sudary of St. Veronica' (Plate 37) might be considered a self-portrait. We follow the suggestions of others and will take as a basis for the identification of self-portraits the St. Luke in the Cathedral of Toledo (Plate 142); from this we can trace the elements of self-portraiture in certain other paintings of apostles (e.g. Plate 143) and likewise in representations of St. Joseph (e.g. Plate 81, also Plate 123 and perhaps Plate 104). To these must be added the earliest and the latest representations (Plates 1 and 141) with their marked physiognomic resemblance.

Plate 5 : The woodcut portrait of Giulio Clovio in the third edition of Vasari's *Vite* (Bologna 1647, Vol. II, 2, p. 259) appears to be based on this painting.

Plate 6 : The drawing was in the collection of Vasari, who inscribed it at the bottom in pen and bistre. It reproduces a lost model by Michelangelo for the "Day" in the Medici Chapel. Numerous similar perspective studies after lost models of Michelangelo were made by Tintoretto.

Plate 7 : Described in the inventory of 1708 as by Giulio Clovio. Another copy of about the same size and Neapolitan in character, is in the possession of Mrs. Charles Shipman Payson, New York. This study is used in Greco's so-called 'Spanish Proverb', the best (signed) copy of which is in the collection of the Earl of Harewood. The same model appears to have been employed in the Santo Domingo altar-piece (cf. Plate 18).

Plate 8 : A larger and likewise unsigned copy belongs to the Hispanic Society of America. The composition is derived from Michelangelo's Pietà in Florence Cathedral.

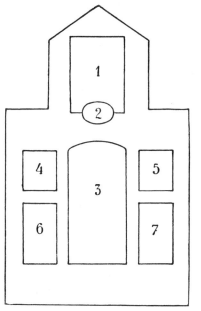

Plate 9 : Signed. The figures on either side are Diego and Antonio Covarrubias.

Plate 10 : Supposed to have been painted in Rome, for Fulvio Orsini, about 1577.

Plates 12, 13, 21, 22, 25, 38, 39 : These belong together. The lower part of the 'Trinity' (Plate 12) was originally covered by the 'Sudary' (Plate 25). The composition of this picture is known to be derived from Dürer's woodcut, 'The Seat of Mercy'. The 'Assumption' (Plate 13) is signed and dated. The Santo Domingo altar in its present state is shown in Calvert's *Toledo,* Plate 480. The original arrangement of the altar is shown in the sketch on the left.

THE HIGH ALTAR OF SANTO DOMINGO EL ANTIGUO. 1. *Holy Trinity* (Plate 12). – 2. *Sudary of St. Veronica* (Plate 25). – 3. *Assumption of the Virgin* (Plate 13). – 4. *St. Bernard* (Plate 38). – 5. *St. Benedict* (Plate 39). – 6. *St. John the Baptist* (Plate 21). – 7. *St. John the Evangelist* (Plate 22).

Plates 23–26 : The only surviving sculpture by El Greco's own hand is the relief of 'St. Dominic receiving the Chasuble' in the Cathedral of Toledo (Plate 26). The sculptures decorating the altar of Santo Domingo (Plates 23–25) were executed by Monegro after designs by El Greco. The following are also attributed to him: the statues of Faith, Hope and Charity in the Hospital de la Caridad at Illescas (ill. on page 16); a Risen Christ (Plate 189) and statues of Saints in the Hospital de San Juan Bautista, completed after El Greco's death by his son; a Madonna of the Rosary of 1591, in the parish church of Talavera; and a series of Apostles (one of them reproduced here on Plate 203).

Plate 27 : In the Cathedral Sacristy is a small picture which is said to be earlier than this version, viz. 1579, whereas the large picture is said to date from 1587. There is a signed copy by Jorge Manuel in the Prado. Replicas from various periods are to be found in the following collections: Conte A. Contini Bonacossi, Florence; Barnes Foundation, Merion, U.S.A.; former Cheramy collection, Paris; Institute of Arts, Minneapolis, U.S.A.; Museo de San Vicente, Toledo. The best version in the broad format is in the museum of Lyons.

Plate 52 : Signed. The hand has been completely painted over. Formerly supposed to be a portrait of Juan de Silva, Marques de Montemayor, 'Notario Mayor' of Toledo.

Plate 53 : This portrait is generally dated too early. It is as far advanced in technique as the portrait heads in the 'Burial of Count Orgaz' (Plates 62–64). Cf. also Plate 108.

Plate 54 : The text of the Latin inscription will be found in Stirling-Maxwell, vol. I, p. 336. – A. L. Mayer says: 'The date 1578 in the signature is inexplicable.'

Plates 65–67 : The male portrait is signed on the back. According to A. L. Mayer, the small portrait of Ranuccio Farnese in the Kaiser Friedrich Museum, Berlin, is an early miniature by Greco. El Greco learnt the painting of miniatures from Clovio.

Plate 68 : Signed. A good workshop repetition is in the National Gallery, London.

Plate 70 : The inscription on the pedestal of the column was added by another hand. Julian Romero died in 1578.

Plate 71 : It has been suggested that the Saint is a portrait of Ferdinand of Spain.

Plate 73 : Despite the signature it is doubtful whether the picture is by Greco's own hand. Copies of the St. John and the Virgin, perhaps by Jorge Manuel, are in the possession of the Hispanic Society of America, New York.

Plates 74, 100, 102, 115, 118, 168, 171 : The four large religious paintings in the Prado appear to belong together, viz. the Golgotha, the Baptism, and the Resurrection of Christ, and the Descent of the Holy Ghost (Plates 74, 115, 118, 171). Three other paintings may be related to them, viz. the Adoration of the Shepherds in Bucharest, the Annunciation in Villanueva, and the Assumption of the Virgin in Toledo (Plates 100, 102, 168). The measurements are approximately the same in the Assumption, the Adoration of the Shepherds and the Baptism of Christ; in the Annunciation and the Golgotha; in the Descent of the Holy Ghost and the Resurrection. The individual pictures were thus painted during a period of about twenty years. It has been suggested that at all events a part of these paintings formed the high altar in the church of the Colegio de Dona Maria de Aragon, Madrid. I myself believe, that we have to do with two altar-pieces: the first, consisting of four panels, may be assigned to the period 1596–1600; the second, a triptych, to the period 1604–1612.

Plate 78 : First attributed to El Greco by Adolfo Venturi.

Plate 79 : Another badly cleaned copy was formerly in the collection of Don José Lazaro Galdeano, Madrid.

Plate 80 : There are several other versions not so well preserved as this.

Plate 84 : Signed. A St. Joseph appears to have been painted over at the right. There is a bad unsigned copy with the St. Joseph in the Prado.

Plate 88 : There is another, more softly painted copy, now on loan to the Art Institute of Chicago.

Plate 96 : Antonio Covarrubias died in 1601. A weaker and earlier version is in the Casa del Greco.

Plate 107 : Signed. There is another version, much overpainted, in the Prado.

Plate 109 : A smaller version, signed with initials, is in the possession of the Hispanic Society of America, New York.

Plates 112 and 113 : Painted for the Capilla de San José, Toledo. The original contract is dated November 9, 1597. The third painting, 'St. Joseph and a Child', is still in the chapel at Toledo (see Plate 122).

Plate 115 : There is a small version in the Galleria Corsini, Rome. Cf. the latest version, Plate 204.

Plate 122 : A larger, unsigned replica is in the Capilla de San José, Toledo. Belongs with Plates 112 and 113, which are signed.

Plate 124 : Signed. Several versions have been preserved. There is an early version in Bergamo, derived from a composition by Titian existing only in a woodcut. Another version, likewise early, in the Zuloaga Museum at Zumaya, already shows wide divergences from Titian's compositions.

Plate 126 : Signed. Numerous replicas by the hands of El Greco and others exist.

Plate 131 : The open book bears an inscription from a later hand: L. Cornaro. Aet. suae 100. 1566. – For this reason it has been supposed that this is a portrait of Luigi Cornaro, author of several treatises on the art of growing old. Others have believed it to be a portrait of the Cardinal-Inquisitor Don Gaspar Quiroga. – Two signed and four unsigned versions are known, the best being that in the Frick Collection (Plate 130).

Plate 133 : Signed. The inscription has been deciphered as: Canonicus Bosio.

Plate 135 : Signed. Diego Covarrubias died in 1577. In the Casa del Greco is a hard and timid portrait by a different hand, which was obviously used by Greco as a model. Cf. Plate 96, portrait of Diego's brother, and Plate 9 with portraits of both brothers.

Plates 139 and 140 : Cf. the early version in Plate 3. Numerous replicas and versions exist, the latest being that in San Gines, Madrid.

Plate 144 : There is another, small version in the collection of Conte Contini Bonacossi in Florence.

Plate 145 : In his left hand St. Paul holds his epistle to the Cretans (Paul's Epistle to Titus).

Plates 150, 181 : These two pictures belong together.

Plate 166 : Supposed portrait of Greco's son, who was however at least thirty years old at that time.

Plate 171 : At the top, the second head from the right is Canonicus Bosio (cf. Plate 133).

Plate 174 : See the Prado Catalogue, No. 2819.

Plate 182 : This is a smaller replica of the picture in the Hospital de la Caridad (Plate 181). It belonged once to the painter Jean François Millet, and later to Edgar Degas.

Plate 188 : See Plate 187, which was originally the upper part of this painting.

Plate 189 : See the note to Plates 23–26. Ordered in 1598, but apparently executed much later.

Plate 191 : An earlier version, in the Colegio del Patriarca at Valencia, was engraved by Diego de Astor, 1605. (There exist four other engravings by Diego de Astor after paintings by Greco, of which two are dated 1606 and one 1608.)

Plate 203 : This bust (and another in the same collection) belongs to a series of twelve Apostles, of which seven have been found (see A. L. Mayer, *El Greco Catalogue* 1926, p. 57, No. 24). If the attribution is accepted, the Apostle busts should be dated after El Greco's statues of Saints in the Hospital de Afuera, namely 1610–14.

Plate 204 : The altar-piece for the hospital church of San Juan Bautista (also called Hospital de Afuera) was left unfinished at Greco's death. Besides the Baptism of Christ, there existed at the time a Descent of the Holy Ghost, a Holy Family, a St. Philip and a St. John with the Lamb. All these paintings have disappeared. – Beneath the Baptism of Christ are two landscapes (the only known landscapes by El Greco besides the view of Toledo in New York), but they were completely painted over by his son and have not yet been uncovered.

NOTE ON THE THIRD EDITION

THE preparations for this Greco book were completed three years before A. L. Mayer published his Critical Catalogue. Before the publication of my book in 1938 I enjoyed the ungrudging advice of A. L. Mayer; I had, moreover, the opportunity of consulting the second volume – which was never published and may have been lost – of his Critical Catalogue.

The second issue of my Greco book was a virtually unchanged reprint of the original edition. I had merely omitted some paintings which I had come to consider doubtful, and had added a few important illustrations. These included three sculptures, some portraits and details from portraits, new details of paintings in the Prado, in the Escorial, and in the Hospital de Afuera. Also new reproductions of works cleaned during the previous ten years.

In this third edition, the original text of 1938 is once more reprinted without change. There are however a number of new illustrations, e.g. a drawing in Munich and another in Edinburgh, four sculptures, and further new details and colour plates.

Since this book was first published, two comprehensive works on the painter have appeared: *El Greco*, by M. Legendre and A. Hartmann, London, 1938; and *Dominico Greco*, by José Camón Aznar, two vols., Madrid, 1950. During the preparation of this reprint, these two works have been perused, but not used.

London, 1953   L. G.

THE PLATES

The paintings are on canvas, unless otherwise stated.
Measurements in inches.

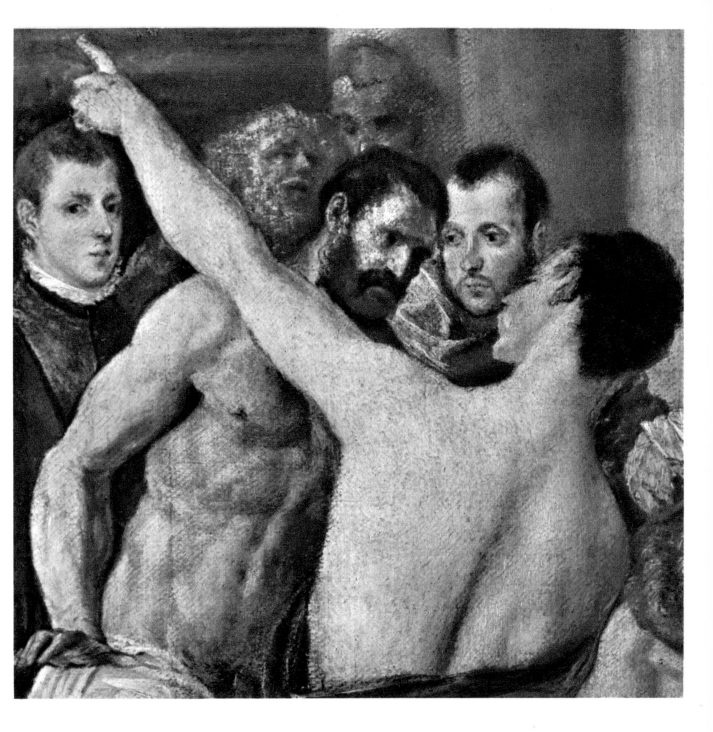

1. FIGURE GROUP FROM THE "HEALING OF THE BLIND MAN" (Plate 2), WITH SELF-PORTRAIT OF THE ARTIST ON THE LEFT. About 1570. ⟨Original size⟩

2. THE HEALING OF THE MAN BORN BLIND. About 1570. Parma, Pinacoteca. ⟨19¾ × 24⟩

3. THE CLEANSING OF THE TEMPLE. About 1572. Minneapolis, U.S.A., Institute of Arts. ⟨56 × 59⟩

4. PORTRAITS OF TITIAN, MICHELANGELO, CLOVIO AND RAPHAEL. Detail from Plate 3. ⟨Reduced about 1 : 1½⟩

5. PORTRAIT OF THE MINIATURE-PAINTER GIULIO CLOVIO. About 1573. Naples, Museo Nazionale. ⟨25⅝ × 37⅜⟩

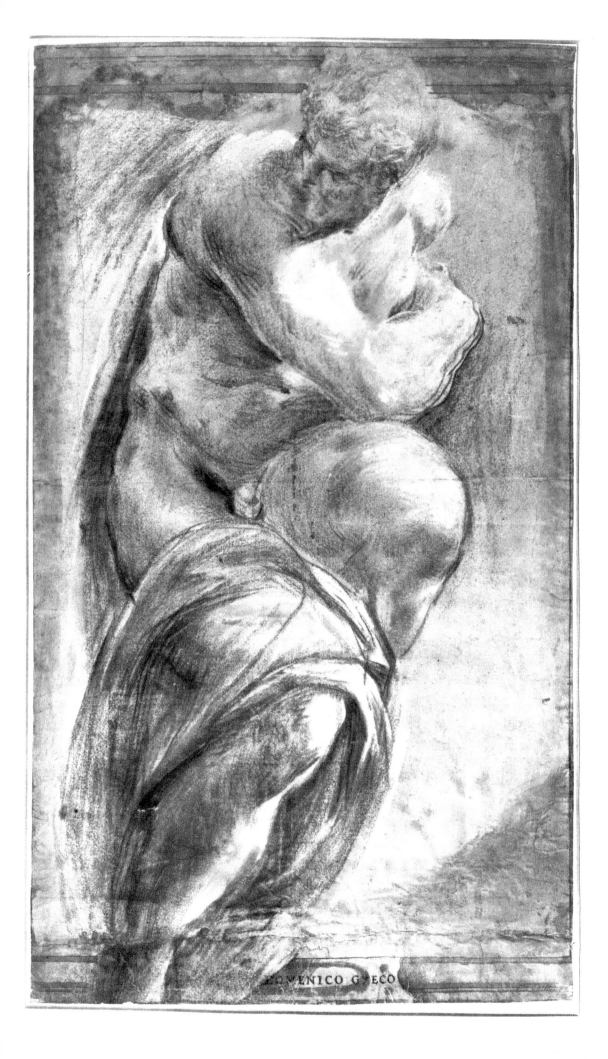

6. STUDY AFTER A LOST MODEL BY MICHELANGELO. Black and white chalk on blue paper. About 1573. Munich, Graphische Sammlung. ⟨23¹/₂ x 13⁵/₈⟩

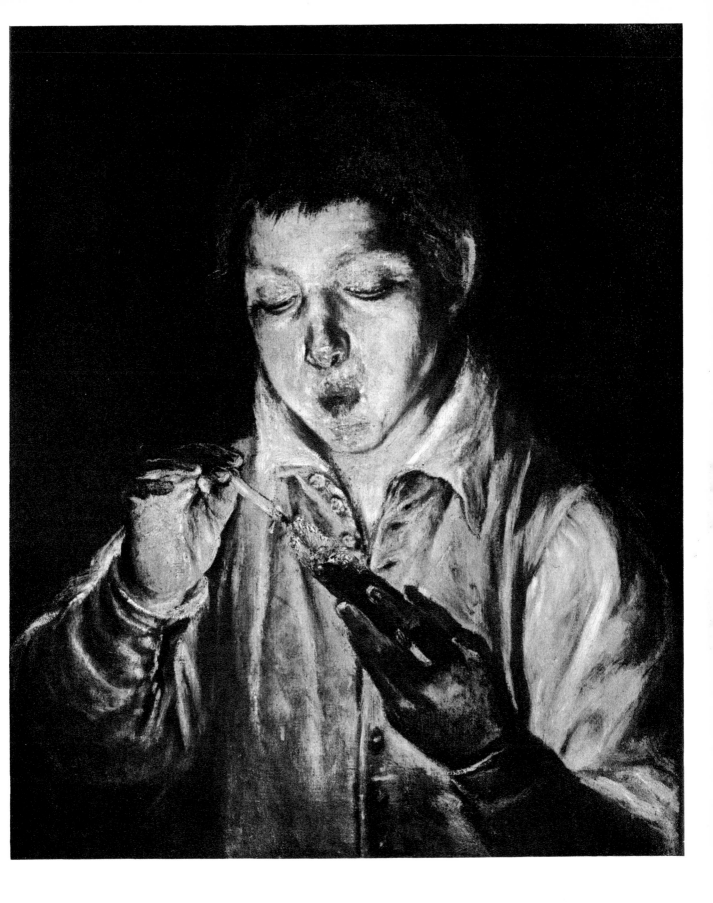

7. YOUTH BLOWING ON CHARCOAL. About 1575. Naples, Museo Nazionale. ⟨25⁵/₈ x 19³/₄⟩

8. PIETA. About 1576. Philadelphia, John G. Johnson Collection. ⟨Wood, 11¹/₂ × 8⟩

9. CHRIST ON THE CROSS, WITH TWO DONORS. About 1577—1580. Paris, Louvre. ⟨98⅜ × 70⅞⟩

10. MOUNT SINAI. About 1577. Formerly Budapest, Baron F. Hatvany. ⟨Wood, 16¹/₈ × 18⁷/₈⟩

11. ST. SEBASTIAN. About 1577. Palencia, Cathedral. ⟨75⅝ × 72½⟩

12. THE HOLY TRINITY. (From the High Altar of Santo Domingo el Antiguo, Toledo.) 1577. Madrid, Prado. ⟨118¹/₈ × 70¹/₂⟩

13. ASSUMPTION OF THE VIRGIN. (Formerly the centre panel of the High Altar of Santo Domingo el Antiguo, Toledo.) 1577. Chicago, Art Institute. ⟨158 x 90⟩

14. RESURRECTION OF CHRIST. 1577. Toledo, Santo Domingo el Antiguo, left transept. ⟨74³/₄ × 48⟩

15. ADORATION OF THE SHEPHERDS. 1577—1579. Toledo, Santo Domingo el Antiguo, right transept. ⟨74³/₄ × 48⟩

16. DETAIL FROM PLATE 15. 〈Reduced about 1 : 1¹/₂〉

17. DETAIL FROM PLATE 15. (Reduced about 1 : 1½)

18. DETAIL FROM PLATE 15. ⟨Reduced about 1 : 1¹/₂⟩

19. PORTRAIT OF DON DIEGO DE CASTILLA. Detail from Plate 14. ⟨Reduced about 1 : 2¹/₂⟩

20. THE PROPHET ISAIAH. Detail from Plate 15. ⟨Reduced about 1 : 2¹/₂⟩

21—22. ST. JOHN THE BAPTIST AND ST. JOHN THE EVANGELIST. 1577—1579. Toledo, Santo Domingo el Antiguo, High Altar. ⟨Each 80³/₄ × 30³/₄⟩

23.—24. TWO SAINTS. 1577—1579. By Monegro from designs by El Greco. Toledo, Santo Domingo el Antiguo. ⟨About 5 ft. high⟩

25. APEX OF THE HIGH ALTAR. 1577—1579. By Monegro from designs by El Greco. Toledo, Santo Domingo el Antiguo. ⟨About 6 ft. wide⟩

26. THE HOLY VIRGIN GIVING THE CHASUBLE TO ST. DOMINIC. Painted wooden relief. 1585. Toledo, Sacristy of the Cathedral. ⟨50×70⟩

27. THE DESPOILING OF CHRIST. 1579 (?). Toledo, Cathedral. ⟨112¹/₈ × 68¹/₈⟩

28. THE DESPOILING OF CHRIST. About 1583. Munich, Ältere Pinakothek. ⟨64 × 39⟩

29. DETAIL FROM PLATE 27. (Reduced about 1 : 5)

30. DETAIL FROM PLATE 27. ⟨Reduced about 1 : 2⟩

31. DETAIL FROM PLATE 27. ⟨Reduced about 1 : 2⟩

32. DETAIL FROM PLATE 27. ⟨Reduced about 1 : 2¹/₂⟩

33. DETAIL FROM PLATE 27. ⟨Reduced about 1 : 2⟩

34. DETAIL FROM PLATE 27. (Reduced about 1:2)

35. DETAIL FROM PLATE 27. ⟨Reduced about 1:2⟩

36. DETAIL FROM PLATE 27. ⟨Reduced about 1 : 2⟩

ST. VERONICA WITH THE SUDARY. About 1579. Toledo, Museo de San Vicente. ⟨31¹/₂ x 27¹/₂⟩

38. ST. BERNARD. About 1579. Formerly Paris, Cheramy Collection. ⟨44¹/₈ × 29⟩

39. ST. BENEDICT. About 1579. Madrid, Prado. ⟨45⁷/₈ x 31⁷/₈⟩

40. THE DREAM OF PHILIP II. About 1580. Escorial, Chapter-Hall. ⟨55¹/₈ × 43¹/₄⟩

41. DETAIL FROM PLATE 40 : The damned in the mouth of hell. ⟨Reduced about 2 : 3⟩

42. DETAIL FROM PLATE 40. ⟨Reduced about 1 : 2¹/₂⟩

DETAIL FROM PLATE 44. (Reduced about 1 : 7)

44. MARTYRDOM OF ST. MAURICE AND THE THEBAN LEGION. 1580. Escorial, Chapter-Hall. ⟨174³/₈ × 118⁷/₈⟩

45. DETAIL FROM PLATE 44. ⟨Reduced about 1 : 5⟩

46. DETAIL FROM PLATE 44. ⟨Reduced 1 : 1¹/₂⟩

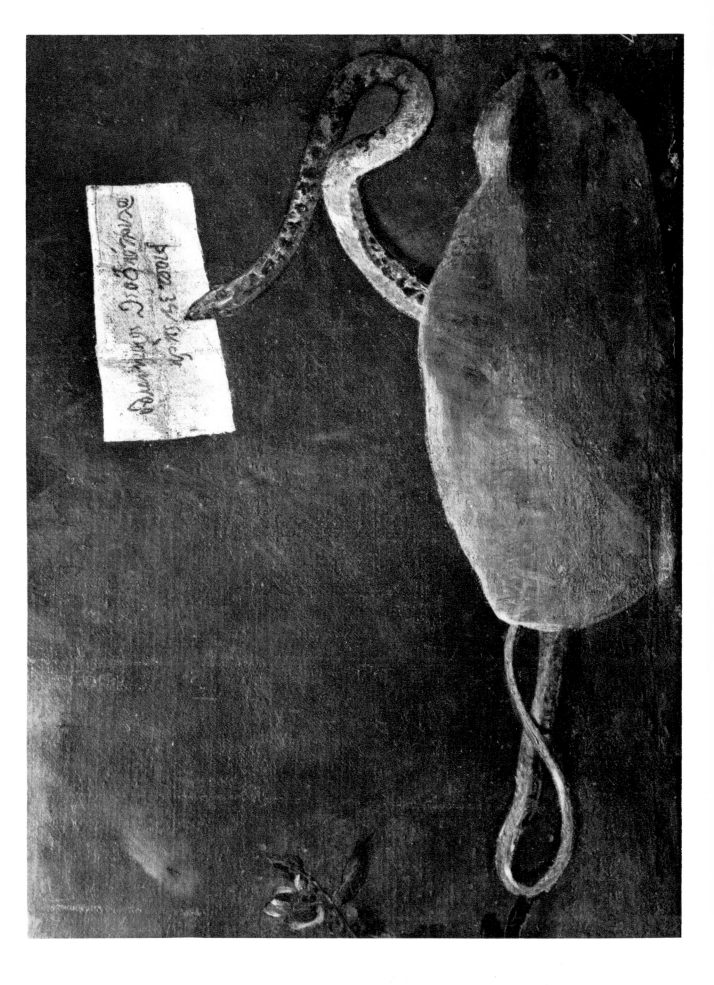

47. DETAIL FROM PLATE 44. ⟨Reduced 1 : 1¹/₂⟩

48. ST. PETER REPENTANT. About 1583. Barnard Castle, Bowes Museum. ⟨41 × 32⟩

49. ST. MARY MAGDALEN REPENTANT. About 1583. Kansas City, U.S.A., William Rockhill Nelson Art Gallery. ⟨41¹/₂ × 33²/₄⟩

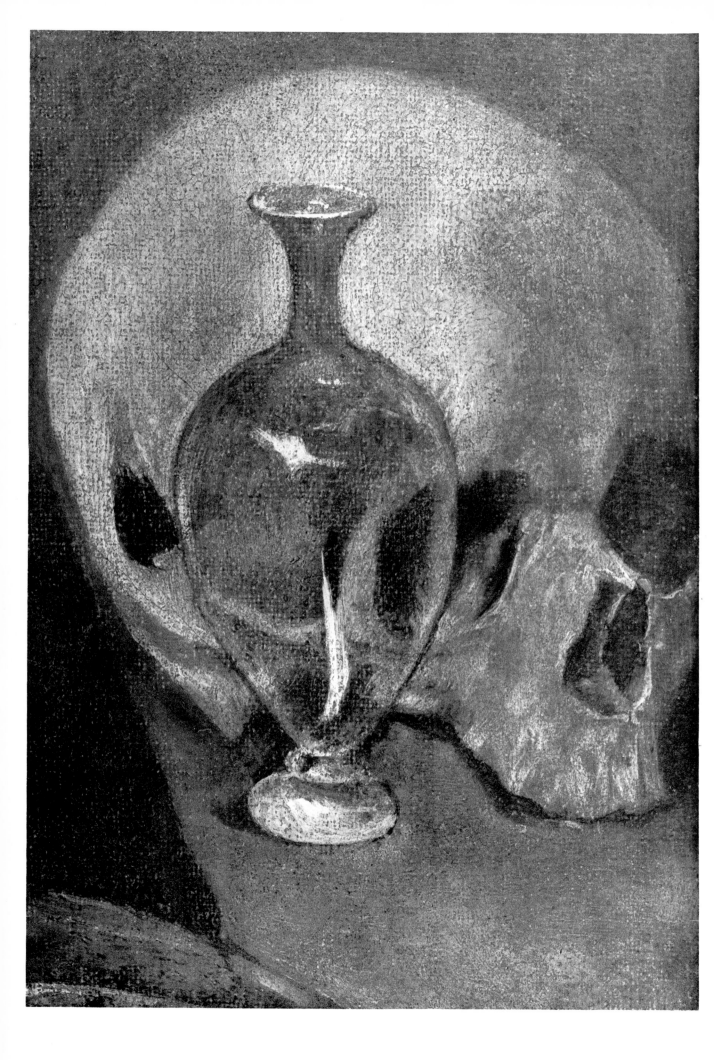

50. DETAIL FROM PLATE 49. ⟨Original size⟩

51. DETAIL FROM PLATE 52 : Sword hilt. ⟨Original size⟩

52. PORTRAIT OF A NOBLEMAN WITH HAND ON BREAST. About 1585. Madrid, Prado. ⟨31⅞ × 26⟩

53. LADY WITH WHITE FOX FUR. (Portrait of Doña Jerónima de las Cuebas ?). About 1585. Glasgow, Stirling-Maxwell Collection. ⟨24⁸/₈ × 20¹/₈⟩

54. BURIAL OF COUNT ORGAZ. 1586. Toledo, San Tomé. ⟨189 × 141³/₄⟩

55. DETAIL FROM PLATE 54 : Saints Stephen and Augustine with the dead Count Orgaz. 〈Reduced about 1 : 5〉

56. DETAIL FROM PLATE 54 : Heads of St. Augustine and Count Orgaz. ⟨Reduced about 1 : 2¹/₂⟩

57. DETAIL FROM PLATE 54 : The Priest Andrés Nuñez. (Reduced about 1 : 4)

58. DETAIL FROM PLATE 54 : Jorge Manuel, the artist's son. ⟨Reduced about 1 : 4¹/₂⟩

59. DETAIL FROM PLATE 58 : The Stoning of St. Stephen. ⟨Reduced about 1 : 3⟩

60. DETAIL FROM PLATE 54 : Head of St. Stephen. ⟨Reduced about 1 : 2¹/₂⟩

61. DETAIL FROM PLATE 54 : Head of a man in the centre of the background. ⟨Reduced about 1 : 2⟩

62. DETAIL FROM PLATE 54 : Head of Jorge Manuel. ⟨Reduced about 1 : 2⟩

63. DETAIL FROM PLATE 54 : Self-portrait of El Greco. (Reduced about 1 : 2)

64. PORTRAIT OF THE DOCTOR AND POET, DON RODRIGO DE LA FUENTE (?). About 1588. Madrid, Prado. ⟨36⁵/₈ × 32¹/₈⟩

65—66. MINIATURE PORTRAITS. About 1588. New York, Hispanic Society of America.
⟨Tempera on paper, original size⟩

67. ENLARGEMENT OF THE FEMALE PORTRAIT.

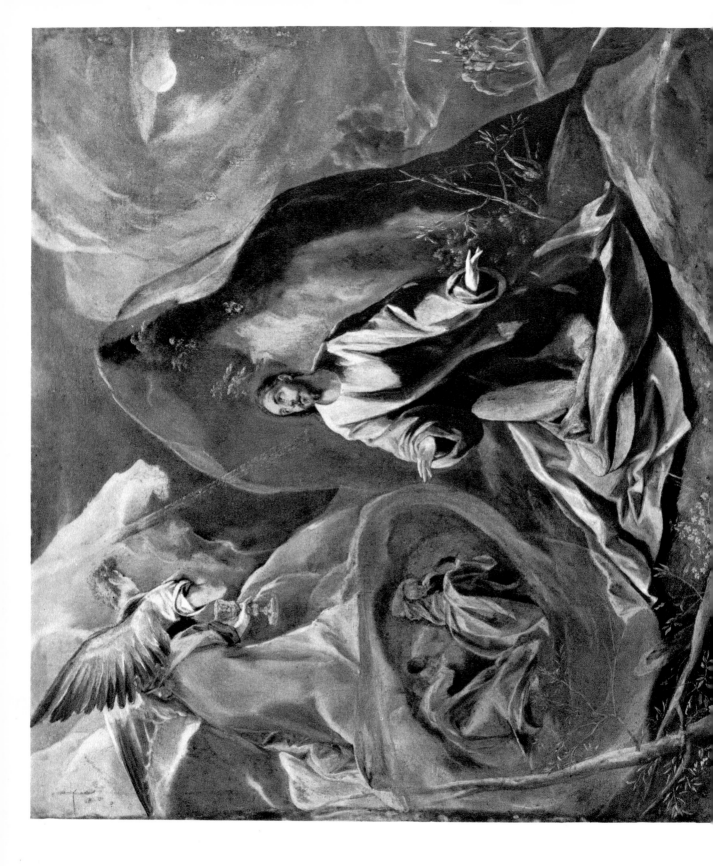

68. CHRIST AT GETHSEMANE. About 1588. Toledo, Ohio, U.S.A., The Toledo Museum of Arts. ⟨41 x 46⟩

69. PIETA. About 1588. Paris, Comtesse de la Béraudière. ⟨47¹/₄ × 57¹/₈⟩

70. PORTRAIT OF JULIAN ROMERO EL DE LAS AZAÑAS WITH HIS PATRON SAINT. About 1588. Madrid, Prado. ⟨81½ × 50⟩

71. ST. LOUIS. About 1588. Paris, Louvre. ⟨46 x 37⅞⟩

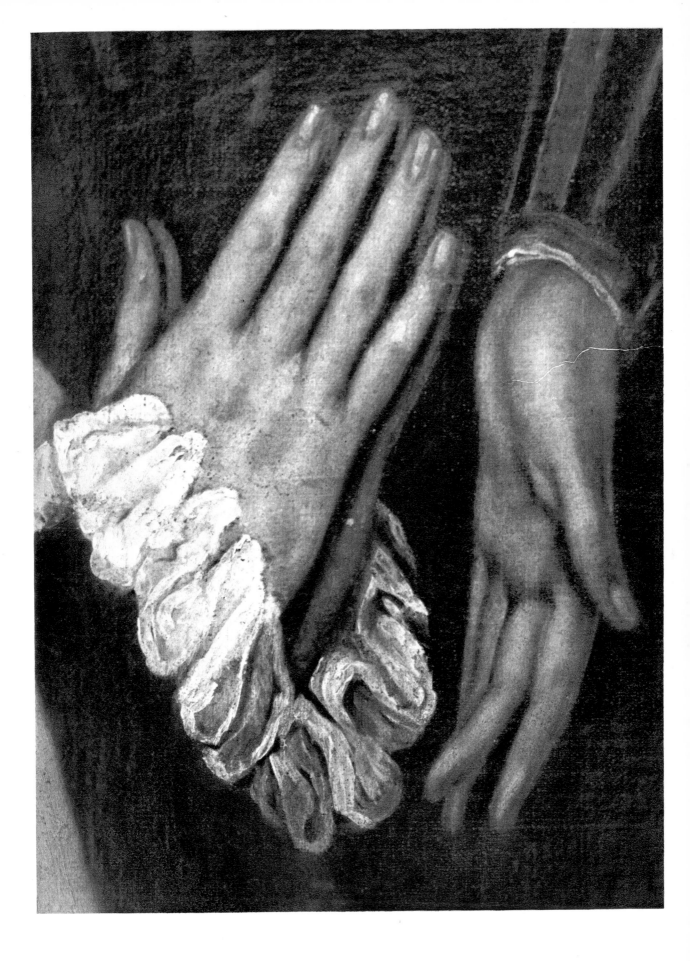

72. DETAIL FROM PLATE 70. ⟨Reduced about 4 : 5⟩

73. CHRIST ON THE CROSS, WITH THE TWO MARIES AND ST. JOHN. About 1588. Athens, Picture Gallery. ⟨47¹/₄ × 31¹/₂⟩

74. GOLGOTHA. About 1590. Madrid, Prado. ⟨122⅞ x 66½⟩

75. DETAIL FROM PLATE 74 : Mater Dolorosa. ⟨Reduced about 1 : 3⟩

76. DETAIL FROM PLATE 74 : St. John. ⟨Reduced about 1 : 3⟩

77. ST. JOHN WITH THE ANGEL. Pen drawing, bistre and wash. About 1590. New York, George Wildenstein. ⟨13³/₈ × 8¹/₈⟩

78. SAINT ANDREW. Pen drawing, wash. About 1590. Edinburgh, National Gallery of Scotland. ⟨12 x 8¹/₂⟩

79. MOURNING MADONNA. About 1590. Lugano, Rohoncz Castle Collection, Thyssen Bequest. ⟨24³/₄ x 18⁷/₈⟩

80. HOLY FAMILY. About 1592. Cleveland, Ohio, U.S.A., The Cleveland Museum of Art. ⟨51¹/₈ × 39³/₈⟩

81. DETAIL FROM PLATE 80 : Self-portrait of the artist (?) as St. Joseph. (Reduced about 1 : 1¹/₂)

82. DETAIL FROM PLATE 80 : Portrait of Doña Jerónima de la Cuebas (?). ⟨Reduced about 1 : 1½⟩

83. DETAIL FROM PLATE 80. ⟨Reduced about 1 : 1¹/₂⟩

84. HOLY FAMILY. About 1592. Toledo, Museo de San Vicente. ⟨63 × 38³/₈⟩

85. DETAIL FROM PLATE 84. ⟨Reduced about 1 : 3⟩

86. FEMALE PORTRAIT. About 1592. Keir, Scotland, Captain Stirling-Maxwell. ⟨26 × 19³/₄⟩

87. PORTRAIT OF A PAINTER. About 1592. Seville, Museo Provincial. ⟨31⁷/₈ × 22⟩

88. CHRIST TAKING LEAVE OF HIS MOTHER. About 1592. Sinaia, Pelishor Castle, Roumania. ⟨24 × 21⟩

89. ST. PETER AND ST. PAUL. About 1592. Barcelona, Luis Plandiura. ⟨47¼ × 36¼⟩

90. ST. PETER AND ST. PAUL. About 1592. Leningrad, Hermitage. ⟨49¹/₄ × 36¹/₂⟩

91. ST. PETER AND ST. PAUL. About 1592. Stockholm, National Museum. ⟨48 × 41⟩

92. DETAIL FROM PLATE 91 : The right hands of St. Peter and St. Paul. ⟨Reduced about 2 : 3⟩

93. DETAIL FROM PLATE 91 : St. Paul. ⟨Reduced about 2 : 3⟩

94. PORTRAIT OF AN UNKNOWN MAN. About 1594. Madrid, Prado. ⟨25¼ x 20⟩

95. PORTRAIT OF A SCHOLAR. About 1594. Amiens, Musée de Picardie. ⟨29 × 18⟩

96. PORTRAIT OF DON ANTONIO DE COVARRUBIAS. About 1594. Toledo, Greco Museum. ⟨26³/₄ × 22⟩

97. PORTRAIT OF A NOBLEMAN. About 1594. New York, Pierre Wertheimer. ⟨20 × 13⟩

98. PORTRAIT OF AN UNKNOWN MAN. About 1594. Madrid, Prado. ⟨18¹/₈ x 16⁷/₈⟩

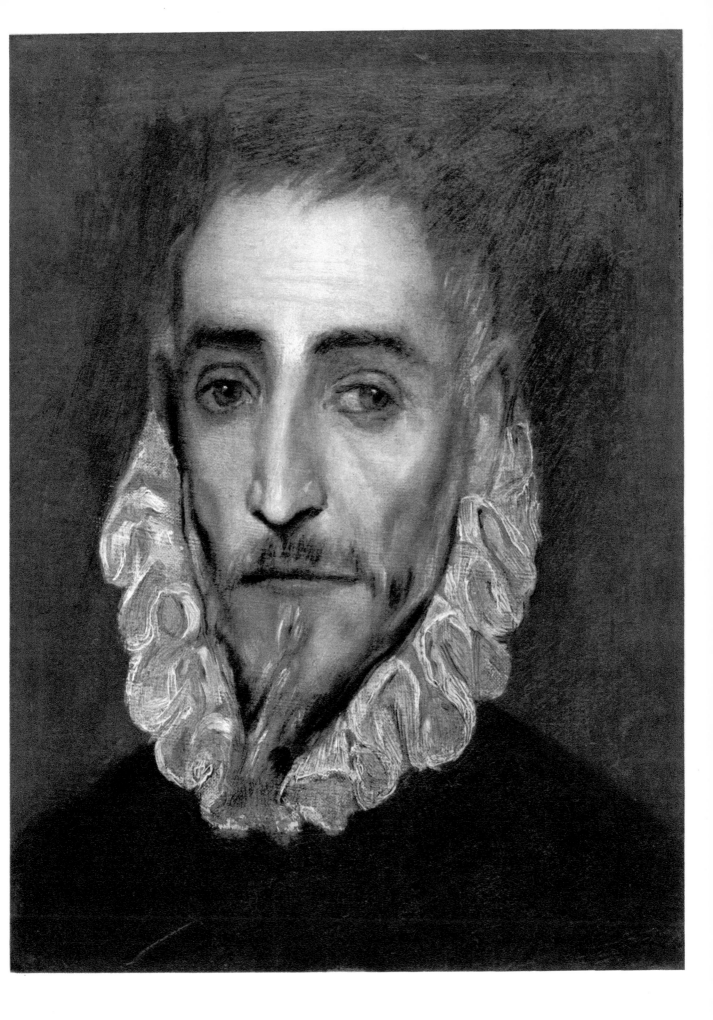

99. PORTRAIT OF AN UNKNOWN MAN. About 1594. New York, Dr. F. Hirschland. ⟨15¹/₂ × 11¹/₂⟩

100. ADORATION OF THE SHEPHERDS. About 1595. Bucharest, Royal Palace. ⟨136¼ × 54⟩

101. DETAIL FROM PLATE 100. ⟨Reduced about 1 : 5⟩

102. ANNUNCIATION. About 1595. Villanueva y Geltru, Museo Biblioteca Balaguer. ⟨124³/₈ × 66⁷/₈⟩

103. DETAIL FROM PLATE 102 : Madonna. (Reduced about 1 : 2¹/₂)

104. HEAD OF ST. MAURICE (or Joseph ?). Fragment. About 1595. Montreal, Canada, Sir William van Horne. ⟨9⁷/₈ × 7⁷/₈⟩

105. SELF-PORTRAIT OF EL GRECO AS THE APOSTLE JAMES THE LESS. About 1595.
Formerly Budapest, Collection of Baron André Herzog de Csete. ⟨21⅜ x 17¾⟩

106. CARRYING OF THE CROSS. About 1595. Madrid, Prado. ⟨42½ x 34⅝⟩

107. MATER DOLOROSA. About 1595. Strasbourg, Municipal Museum. ⟨20⁷/₈ x 14¹/₂⟩

108. FEMALE PORTRAIT. Portrait of Doña Jerónima de las Cuebas (?). About 1595. Philadelphia, John G. Johnson Collection. ⟨15³/₄ × 13⟩

109. ST. JAMES THE GREAT. About 1595. Formerly Budapest, Baron André Herzog de Csete. ⟨36³/₄ x 18¹/₂⟩

110. ST. ILDEFONSO. About 1597. Escorial, Sacristy. ⟨87³/₈ × 41³/₈⟩

111. MADONNA ON THRONE OF CLOUDS. About 1597. Barcelona, Luis Rey. ⟨11½ x 7⅞⟩

112. MADONNA ON THRONE OF CLOUDS WITH SAINTS AGNES AND MARINA. About 1597.
(From the Capilla de San José, Toledo.) Washington, National Gallery of Art, Widener Collection. ⟨75¼ × 38⅝⟩

113. ST. MARTIN. About *1597*. (From the Capilla de San José, Toledo.) Washington,
National Gallery of Art, Widener Collection. ⟨75¼ x 38⅝⟩

114. ST. MARTIN. About 1604. Washington, National Gallery of Art, Mellon Collection. (41 × 23½)

115. BAPTISM OF CHRIST. About 1598. Madrid, Prado. ⟨137³/₄ × 56²/₄⟩

116. DETAIL FROM PLATE 115. ⟨Reduced about 1 : 4⟩

117. DETAIL FROM PLATE 115. ⟨Reduced about 1 : 4¹/₂⟩

118. RESURRECTION OF CHRIST. About 1598. Madrid, Prado. ⟨108¹/₄ × 50⟩

119. DETAIL FROM PLATE 118. ⟨Reduced about 1 : 4⟩

120. DETAIL FROM PLATE 118. ⟨Reduced about 1 : 4⟩

121. DETAIL FROM PLATE 118. ⟨Reduced about 1 : 4⟩

122. ST. JOSEPH WITH THE CHILD JESUS. About 1598. Toledo, Museo de San Vicente. ⟨42⁷/₈ × 21⁵/₈⟩

123. DETAIL FROM PLATE 122. ⟨Original size⟩

124. ST. FRANCIS WITH BROTHER RUFUS. About 1598. Cadiz, Hospital de Mujeres. ⟨79⁷/₈ × 49¹/₄⟩

125. DETAIL FROM PLATE 124 : Brother Rufus. ⟨Reduced about 1 : 4⟩

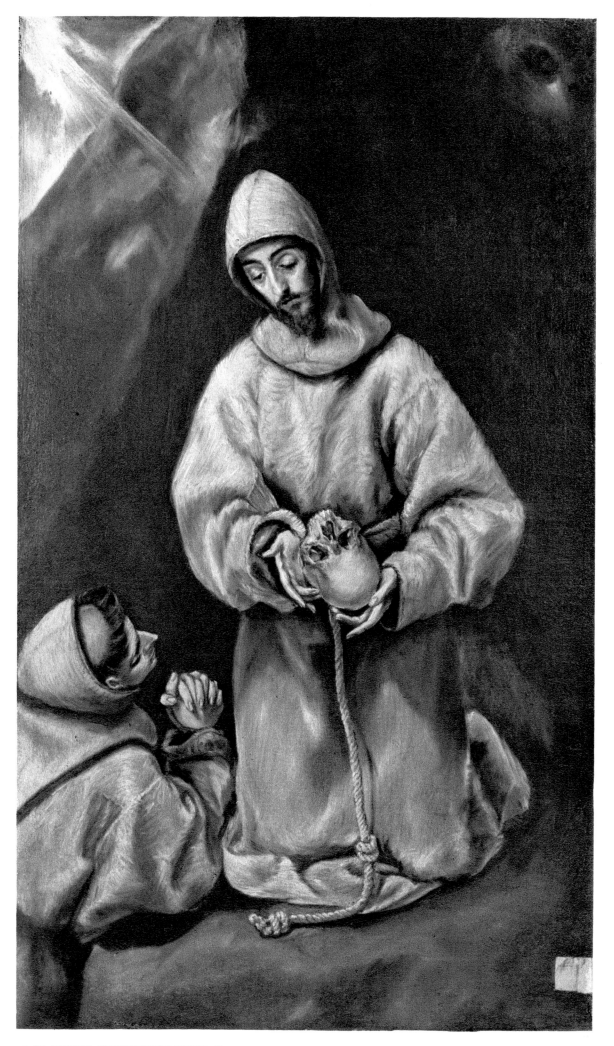

126. ST. FRANCIS WITH BROTHER RUFUS. About 1598. Milan, Brera. ⟨43¼ x 26⅜⟩

127. ST. FRANCIS. (Cf. Plate 126.) Detail from the version in Toledo Cathedral. ⟨Original size⟩

128. BROTHER RUFUS. (Cf. Plate 126.) Detail from the version in possession of Professor Albert Hahn, Porto Ronco. (Reduced about 1 : 1½)

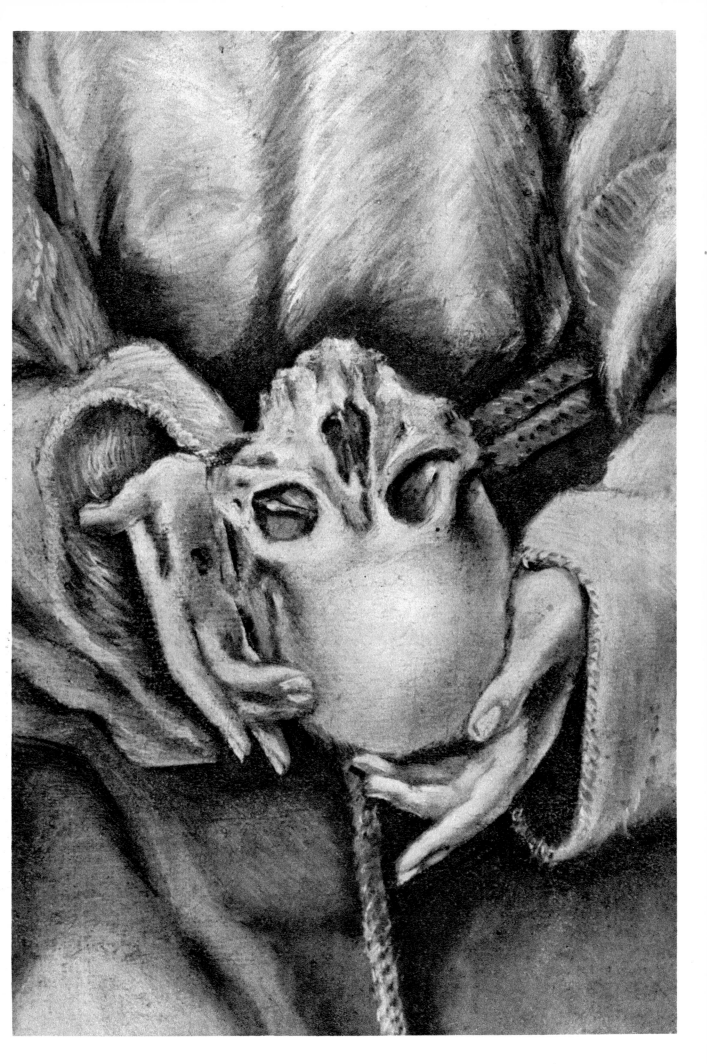

129. HANDS AND SKULL. (Cf. Plate 126.) Detail from the version in the possession of Professor Albert Hahn, Porto Ronco. ⟨Reduced about 1 : 1½⟩

130. ST. JEROME AS CARDINAL. About 1600. New York, Frick Collection. ⟨42¹/₈ × 34¹/₄⟩

131. ST. JEROME AS CARDINAL. About 1600. London, National Gallery. ⟨23 × 18½⟩

132. PORTRAIT OF DON RODRIGO VAZQUEZ. About 1604. Madrid, Prado. ⟨24³/₈ x 16¹/₂⟩

133. PORTRAIT OF CANONICUS BOSIO. About 1604. Sinaia, Pelesh Castle, Roumania. ⟨45⁵/₈ × 33⁷/₈⟩

134. PORTRAIT OF CARDINAL TAVERA. About 1604. Toledo, Hospital de San Juan Bautista. ⟨40¼ × 32⅝⟩

137. DETAIL FROM PLATE 136. (Reduced about 1 : 1¹/₂)

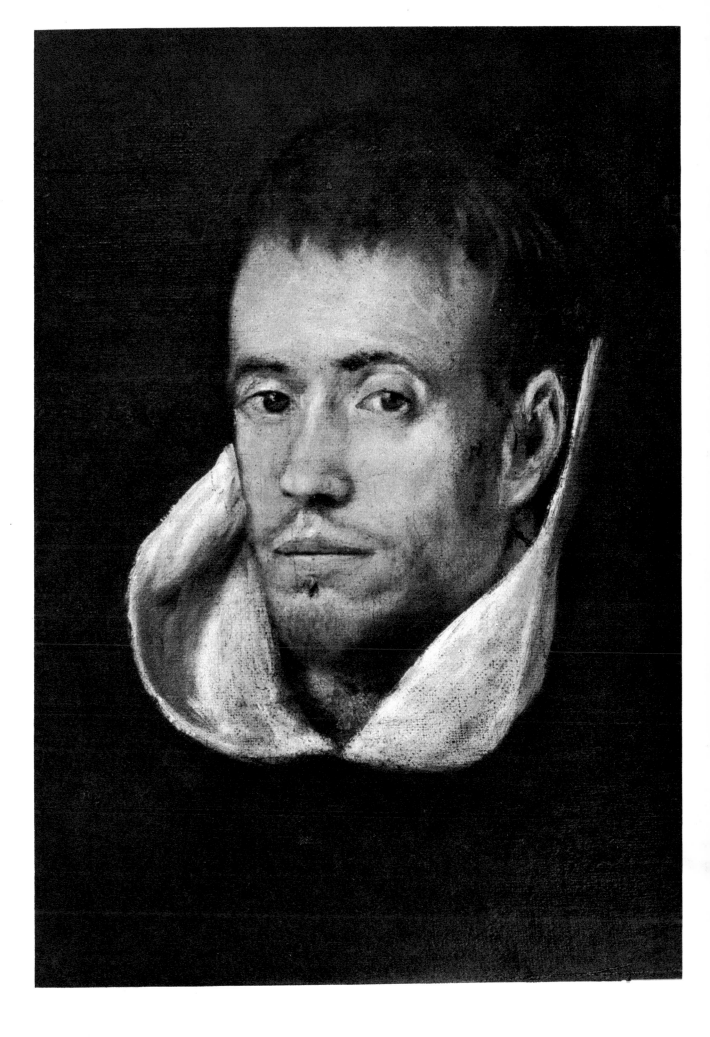

138. PORTRAIT OF A DOMINICAN. About 1604. Madrid, Prado. ⟨14 x 10¹/₂⟩

139. THE CLEANSING OF THE TEMPLE. About 1604. Cambridge, Mass., U.S.A., Fogg Art Museum. ⟨17 × 21⟩

140. THE CLEANSING OF THE TEMPLE. About 1604. London, National Gallery. ⟨41³/₈ × 50⟩

141. SELF-PORTRAIT OF THE ARTIST. About 1604. New York, Metropolitan Museum. ⟨23¼ × 18⅛⟩

142. ST. LUKE. About 1604. Toledo, Cathedral. ⟨38⅝ x 30¾⟩

143. ST. SIMON. About 1604. New York, Hispanic Society of America. (28 × 21)

144. ST. PHILIP. About 1604. Madrid, Prado. ⟨27¹/₂ × 22⟩

145. ST. PAUL. About 1604. St. Louis, Missouri, City Art Museum. ⟨27¹/₂ × 22⟩

146. ST. THOMAS. About 1604. Toledo, Cathedral. ⟨38⅝ x 30¾⟩

147. ST. JOHN THE EVANGELIST. About 1604. Madrid, Prado. ⟨35 × 30¼⟩

148. ST. DOMINIC. About 1604. Toledo, Museo de San Vicente. ⟨39 × 21⅝⟩

149. ST. DOMINIC. About 1604. Toledo, Cathedral. ⟨47¼ × 22⅞⟩

150. MADONNA CARITATIS. About 1606. Illescas, Hospital de la Caridad. (61 x 43³/₄)

151. ST. BERNARD OF SIENA. About 1606. Toledo, Greco Museum. ⟨106 x 56¾⟩

152. DETAIL FROM PLATE 150. ⟨Original size⟩

153. DETAIL FROM PLATE 151. ⟨Reduced about 1 : 2¹/₂⟩

154. ST. BARTHOLOMEW. About 1606. Toledo, Greco-Museum. ⟨38⅝ × 30¾⟩

5. ST. ANDREW. About 1606. Toledo, Cathedral. ⟨38⅝ × 30¾⟩

156. DETAIL FROM PLATE 154. ⟨Reduced about 1 : 1,7⟩

157. DETAIL FROM PLATE 155. ⟨Reduced about 1 : 1¹/₂⟩

158. ST. PETER. About 1606. Escorial, Sacristy. ⟨81¹/₂ × 41³/₈⟩

159. CHRIST. About 1606. Toledo Cathedral. ⟨38⁵/₈ × 30³/₄⟩

160. CHRIST IN THE HOUSE OF SIMON THE PHARISEE. About 1608. Havanna, Cuba, The Hon. Oscar B. Cintas. ⟨58 x 40⟩

161. CHRIST IN THE HOUSE OF SIMON THE PHARISEE. About 1608. Burlington, Vermont, U.S.A., Joseph Winterbothom. ⟨57 × 40³/₄⟩

162. GOLGOTHA. About 1606. Philadelphia, John G. Johnson Collection. ⟨62⅝ x 38¾⟩

163. GOLGOTHA. About 1608. Cincinnati, Ohio, U.S.A., Cincinnati Art Museum. ⟨41 × 24³/₅⟩

164. DETAIL FROM PLATE 163 : View of Toledo. ⟨Reduced about 1 : 1¹/₂⟩

165. TOLEDO. About 1608. New York, Metropolitan Museum. ⟨47⅝ × 41¾⟩

166. VIEW AND PLAN OF TOLEDO. About 1608. Toledo, Greco Museum. ⟨53¹/₈ × 89³/₄⟩

167. DETAIL FROM PLATE 166. ⟨Reduced about 1 : 2⟩

168. ASSUMPTION OF THE VIRGIN. About 1608. Toledo, Museo de San Vicente. ⟨128 x 66⁷/₈⟩

171. DESCENT OF THE HOLY GHOST. About 1608. Madrid, Prado. ⟨108¹/₄ x 50⟩

172. CHRIST ON THE MOUNT OF OLIVES. About 1608. Formerly Budapest, Baron André Herzog de Csete. ⟨66⅞ × 44⅛⟩

173. ST. ANDREW. About 1608. Paris, unknown private collection.

174. ST. ANDREW AND ST. FRANCIS. About 1608. Madrid, Prado. ⟨65³/₄ × 44¹/₂⟩

175. ST. JOHN THE EVANGELIST AND ST. FRANCIS. About 1608. Madrid, Prado. ⟨25¼ x 19¾⟩

176. THE TWO SAINTS JOHN. About 1608. Toledo, Church of the Jesuits. ⟨42⁷/₈ × 33¹/₂⟩

177. DETAIL FROM PLATE 176 : St. John the Evangelist. ⟨Reduced about 1 : 1¹/₂⟩

178. DETAIL FROM PLATE 176 : St. John the Baptist. ⟨Reduced about 1 : 1½⟩

179. ST. AUGUSTINE. About 1608. Toledo, Museo de San Vicente. ⟨49¼ × 17⅞⟩

180. THE VISION OF ST. DOMINIC. About 1608. New York, Rochester Art Gallery. ⟨39¼ x 24⟩

181. ST. ILDEFONSO. About 1608. Illescas, Hospital de la Caridad. ⟨62 x 40⟩

182. ST. ILDEFONSO. About 1608. Washington, National Gallery of Art, Mellon Collection. ⟨44¼ x 25¾⟩

183. DETAIL FROM PLATE 181 : St. Ildefonso. ⟨Reduced about 1 : 2⟩

184. PORTRAIT OF FRAY HORTENSIO FELIX PARAVICINO. 1609. Boston, Museum of Fine Arts. ⟨43¼ × 33⟩

185. PORTRAIT OF A HIDALGO. About 1609. Minneapolis, U.S.A., Institute of Arts. ⟨42¹/₂ × 33⁷/₈⟩

186. DETAIL FROM PLATE 103 : ANGELIC CONCERT. ⟨Reduced about 1 : 6½⟩

187. ANGELIC CONCERT. About 1610. (Originally the upper part of the " Annunciation " belonging to the Marqués de Urquijo, Plate 188.) Athens, Picture Gallery ⟨45¼ × 85½⟩

188. ANNUNCIATION. About 1610. Madrid, Marqués de Urquijo. ⟨96 x 85¹/₂⟩

189. THE RISEN CHRIST. After a design by El Greco. About 1610. Toledo, Hospital de San Juan Bautista (Hospital de Afuera). ⟨17³/₄″ high⟩

190. ADORATION OF THE SHEPHERDS. Detail. Valencia, Colegio del Patriarca. ⟨Reduced about 1 : 2⟩
(A later variant is in the Metropolitan Museum, New York ; Plate 191.)

191. ADORATION OF THE SHEPHERDS. About 1610. New York, Metropolitan Museum. (64¹/₂ × 42)

192. PORTRAIT OF AN OLD MAN. About 1610. Florence, Conte A. Contini-Bonacossi. ⟨18⁷/₈ x 15²/₈⟩

193. LAOCOÖN. About 1610. Washington, National Gallery of Art, Kress Collection. ⟨55⅞ × 76⟩

194. THE OPENING OF THE FIFTH SEAL. About 1610. Zumaya, Museo Zuloaga. ⟨88¼ × 76⅜⟩

197. DETAIL FROM PLATE 194. ⟨Reduced about 1 : 4¹/₂⟩

98. DETAIL FROM PLATE 204. (Reduced about 1 : 1½)

199. VISITATION OF THE VIRGIN. About 1612—1614. Washington, Dumbarton Oaks Collection. ⟨38¹/₄ × 28¹/₄⟩

200. BETROTHAL OF THE VIRGIN. 1614. (Unfinished.) Sinaia, Foishor Castle, Roumania. ⟨43¹/₄ × 32⁵/₈⟩

201. DETAIL FROM PLATE 200. ⟨Approximately original size⟩

202. DETAIL FROM PLATE 200 : Self-portrait of El Greco. (Approximately orginal size)

203. BUST OF AN APOSTLE. Unpainted wood, about 1612—1614. Lugano, Rohoncz Castle Collection, Thyssen Bequest. ⟨19 high⟩

204. BAPTISM OF CHRIST. 1612—1614. Toledo, Hospital de San Juan Bautista. ⟨162 × 37½⟩

205. ST. FRANCIS. About 1612—1614. Toledo, Hospital de San Juan Bautista. ⟨34 × 28⟩

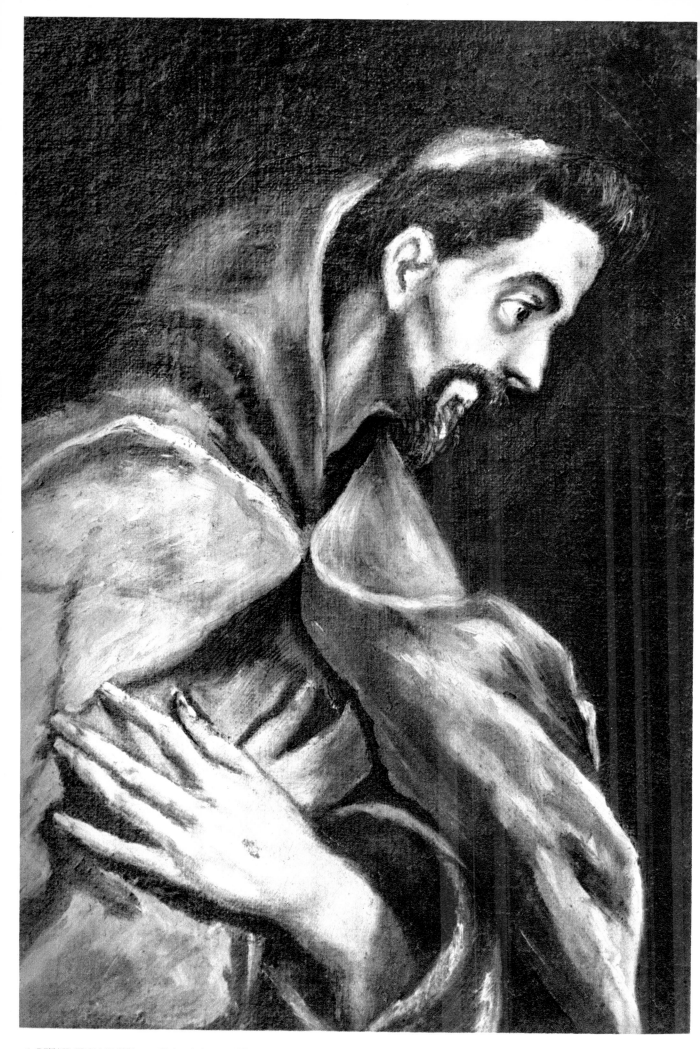

206. DETAIL FROM PLATE 205. ⟨Reduced about 1 : 1½⟩

207. DETAIL FROM PLATE 204. ⟨Reduced about 1 : 1¹/₂⟩

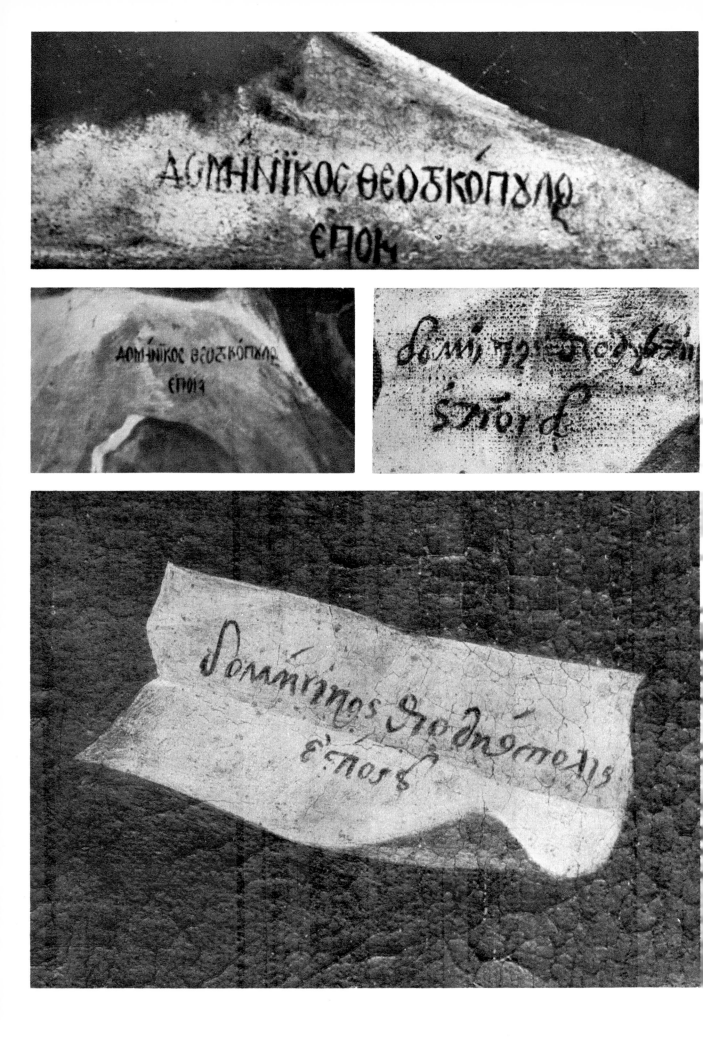

208. SIGNATURES OF EL GRECO. Above : about 1577. Centre, left : about 1580. Centre, right : about 1586. Below : about 1595.

BIBLIOGRAPHY
INDEX OF COLLECTIONS
AND INDEX OF SUBJECTS

CONCISE BIBLIOGRAPHY

MONOGRAPHS

Pietro Martini: Del pittore Domenico Theotocopulo e di suo dipinto. Turin 1862

M. D. Bikelas: A Study of El Greco. Athens 1894

Carl Justi: El Greco (in 'Zeitschrift für Bildende Kunst'). Leipzig 1897

Miguel Utrillo: Domenico Theotocopulos. Barcelona 1906

Manuel B. Cossío: El Greco. Madrid 1908

Carl Justi: Miscellaneen aus drei Jahrhunderten spanischen Kunstlebens. Berlin 1908. (With two chapters on El Greco)

Maurice Barrès und Paul Lafond: Le Greco. Paris 1911 (new edition 1931)

August L. Mayer: El Greco. Munich 1911 (third edition 1920)

Ricardo Jorge: El Greco. Coimbra 1912

Maurice Barrès: Greco, ou le secret de Toledo. Paris 1912 (Neudruck 1923)

Paul Lafond: Le Greco. Paris 1913

Miguel de Unamuno: Il Greco (in 'Rassegna d'Arte'). Rome 1914

A. de Beruete y Moret: El Greco, pintor de retratos. Toledo 1914

H. Kehrer: Die Kunst des Greco. Munich 1914

August L. Mayer: El Greco. Kritisches und illustriertes Verzeichnis des Gesamtwerks. Munich 1926. (The second volume remained unprinted)

J.-F. Willumsen: La jeunesse du Greco. Paris 1927

August L. Mayer: El Greco. Berlin 1931

WORKS CONTAINING INFORMATION ON EL GRECO'S LIFE AND ART

Elias Tormo: The natal country of El Greco (in El Debate, 8 February 1935)

Manuel B. Cossío: Lo que se sabe de la vida del Greco. Madrid 1914

Natalia Cossio de Jimenez: Notes on Greco's birthplace, education and family. Oxford 1948. (With references to Greco literature 1939–1947)

Don Francisco de Borja de San Román y Fernández: El Greco en Toledo. Madrid 1910 (new edition 1916)

Don Francisco de Borja de San Román y Fernández: De la vida del Greco. Nueva serie de documentos inéditos (in 'Archivo español de arte y arqueología' No. 8 and 9, 1927)

Don Diego Ponz: Viaje de España. Madrid 1776

Elie Lambert: Les procédés du Greco (in 'Gazette des Beaux-Arts'). Paris 1921

Juan Moraleda y Esteban: Dos Grecos más en Toledo. Toledo 1910

Narciso Sentenach y Cabañas: Técnica pictórica del Greco ('Sociedad española de excursiones', Boletín. März 1916, Vol. XXIV)

Jerónimo López Cedillo Conde de Ayala: De la religiosidad y del misticismo en las obras del Greco. Madrid 1915

Kurt Steinbart: Greco und die spanische Mystik (in 'Repertorium für Kunstwissenschaft', 36, 121 f.)

A. Goldschmidt: Grecos Augenkrankheit (in 'Süddeutsche Monatshefte'). Munich 1911

Germán Beritens: Aberraciones del Greco cientificamente consideradas. Madrid 1913

Germán Beritens: El astigmatismo del Greco. Madrid 1914

Don Francisco de Borja de San Román y Fernández: El sepulcro de los Theotocopulos. Madrid 1912

EXHIBITIONS AND COLLECTIONS

Salvador Viniegra: Catálogo ilustrado de la exposición de las obras de Domenico Theotocopulos. Madrid 1902

J. Lacoste: Catálogo ilustrado de las obras de Domenico Theotocopulos. Madrid 1902

Al. Busuioceanu: Les tableaux du Greco dans la Collection Royale de Roumanie. Paris 1937

Georges Wildenstein: El Greco, Catalogue de l'Exposition organisée par la 'Gazette des Beaux-Arts'. Paris 1937

TOLEDO

Amador de los Rios: Toledo pintoresca. Madrid 1845

R. Ramírez de Arellano: Catálogo de artífices que trabajaron en Toledo, y cuyos nombres y obras aparecen en los archivos de sus parroquías. Toledo 1920

R. Ramírez de Arellano: Notas del archivo de la catedral de Toledo. Madrid 1914

SPANISH PAINTING

Francisco Pacheco: Arte de Pintura. Sevilla 1649.

Don Antonio Palomino de Castro y Velasco: El Museo Pictórico y Escala Optica. Madrid 1724 (1796)

Richard Cumberland: Anecdotes of Eminent Painters in Spain. London 1782

Richard Cumberland: Catalogue of the several Paintings in the King of Spain's Palace at Madrid. London 1787

Sir William Stirling-Maxwell: Annals of the Artists of Spain. New edition. London 1891

Valerian von Loga: Die Malerei in Spanien. Berlin 1923

August L. Mayer: Pintura Española. Barcelona 1926. (There is also a two-volume edition in German, Leipzig 1913; new impression 1922)

Don Francisco de Borja de San Roman y Fernandez: El Greco en Toledo. Madrid 1910

INDEX OF MUSEUMS AND COLLECTIONS

INDEX OF SUBJECTS